Goo

Coping with bereavement

W Sydney Callaghan

First published in Great Britain in
1990 by Fount Paperbacks, an
inprint of HarperCollinsReligious

First Colourpoint Books edition 1999
This second edition published by Colourpoint Books, 2003
© W Sydney Callaghan
  1999

ISBN 1 904242 18 9

6 5 4 3 2

Designed by Colourpoint Books
Printed by Betaprint

Colourpoint Books
Unit D5 Ards Business Centre
Jubilee Road
Newtownards
Co Down
BT23 4YH
Tel: 028 9182 0505
Fax: 028 9182 1900
E-mail: info@colourpoint.co.uk
Web-site: www.colourpoint.co.uk

About the Author

The Rev W Sydney Callaghan says he "was born in Dublin in the South, lives in Belfast in the North, but Ireland is his home". Educated at High School, he is a graduate of Trinity College, Dublin. He studied for the ministry of the Methodist Church in Edgehill College, Belfast and has done post-graduate work in Queen's University where subsequently he was part of the lecturing team in the Department of Mental Health, the Department of General Practice and in Union and Edgehill Theological Colleges. He has been General Secretary of the Council on Social Responsibility of the Methodist Church in Ireland and one of the longest standing members of the Northern Ireland Mental Health Review Tribunal. He has been a Chaplain in both industry and a hospital setting; was a member of the Eastern Health and Social Services Council and the Professional Conduct Committee of the United Kingdom Central Council for Nursing, Midwifery and Health Visiting. Founder member and later Director of the Samaritans in Belfast and a founder member of the Northern Ireland Hospice of which he was Methodist Chaplain. Board member of Oaklee Housing Association and a Director of the Irish Association of Suicidology, Patron of Dismas House – a hostel for ex-offenders, – Northern Ireland Widows Association and Care for Cancer (Omagh). An active supporter of Mother Teresa's work throughout the world. He was named in the 'People of the Year' award in 1976 for "an outstanding contribution to society in Ireland", and awarded the OBE in the 1984 New Year's Honours List. He was President of the Methodist Church in Ireland 1980-81. He was married and has two children. Sadly he passed away on 23 February 2001 before the publication of this new edition.

For Brenda, Kate and Michael,
still my keenest critics
and
my most loyal supporters

Royalties from the sale of this book will go to

The Samaritans of Belfast
The Northern Ireland Hospice
Mother Frances Dominica
of Helen House, Oxford,
and the continuing work begun
by Mother Teresa of Calcutta

Contents

Preface

IT IS SAID it takes a lot of cheek and a lot of conceit to write a book – cheek to imagine it would be worth reading and conceit to think that anybody would actually read it! It is hoped this writer has neither.

It was born – a not inappropriate metaphor – at a Refresher Course for Midwives. To remain on the Register, a nurse or midwife must attend a Refresher Course every five years. The content is mainly decided by the educators but in part by the students themselves, some of whom said they were grateful for all the up-to-date information and scientific data they received but they had not been given much help to deal with a mother who had just lost a baby or those heartbroken because they couldn't have one or who had suffered a miscarriage. How did the practitioner cope with her feelings on the way home from the Unit when she had to deal with her own children or a husband 'who'd had a bad day at the office' (as though she knew nothing of that sort of experience herself)!

They asked for some guidance. They wanted some input which took on board the feelings and the fears, the hurt and the heartache – something realistic, down to earth not highfalutin' and over the top. So these talks – for that is what they were originally, were put together and 'tried out' on people at the sharp end. They made their input and shared their insights. This little volume is the result. It doesn't purport to be earth-shattering or mind-blowing – that is left to others – but something brief and readable for ordinary people by a very ordinary person who has tried to listen to what others have had to say and learn from them. In that sense it is 'their book' and not 'mine'.

It has been encouraging to find it has met a niche. This is why it has been reprinted with some changes, through helpful suggestions and additional information of a practical variety.

The original has found its way to many parts of the world. Hospice Groups have had it translated into Romanian and Czech. A Consular official in Bombay keeps copies to give to distressed people. A South African minister still uses it with bereaved people. An international athlete stated publicly it and the author had saved her life when overtaken by a personal loss which triggered off unresolved dealings with other losses. A Scottish pastoral theology lecturer recommends it to his students as "the best brief book on the subject" and many colleges of nursing have it on their shelves and use it as an education tool. The Principal of a Divinity School said he experienced all of the feelings spelt out in the book when the college library was destroyed in a fire. A lay preacher says it helped her come to terms with her father's death and she feels she could give it to an atheist without feeling embarrassed! When questioned why, she said so many writing on the theme were either 'dripping with piety' or else so orthodox and traditional that those who found difficulty with belief where made to feel odd. There was no denominational slant or religious megatones but an understanding, compassionate awareness of where different people are along the road.

There was an old lady whose daughter brought her to the other side of the world to cheer her up when her father died. It was a disastrous mistake. The idea was well intentioned but the results terrible – possibly because it was too soon and there was too much baggage from the past. The mother returned home. The upset daughter went one day into a bookshop asking if they had anything suitable which might help. She was directed to an appropriate section and liked the size of the book and because of that and its Irish links she posted it to her mother who read it and re-read it and found in it what she needed, leading to a friendship with the writer which brought new light into her life and has enabled her to live as never before.

Some value it because of its brevity. It can be taken up and left down.It doesn't make too great an intellectual or emotional demand at a time when we are not able to cope with pressures. It isn't daunting but comforting – in small doses which can be just about managed. When given with tender loving care it "can soothe the troubled breast".

The content remains much as it was when first written with the suggested emendations, and cognisance being taken of personal and communal wants, eg. the Omagh tragedy being incorporated into the text along with an additional chapter about trauma.

The hope and prayer with which it was sent on its way nearly a decade ago still sustains it. What possibly helps to justify the new edition is the demand for it – and the ongoing financial benefit to the causes dear to the author's heart. If it continues to help them in a practical way and can ease your pain and hurt it will have been well worth the bother. Thank you for your comments and occasional criticisms. They have enriched my life and brought even greater insights than before. I'm grateful to Evelyn Woods and Deirdre Mooney who typed the original and helped bring it up-to-date; Samaritan colleagues who gathered additional information for the Appendix and Sheila Johnston of Colourpoint Books for helpful suggestions, format and attractive presentation. The credit for quality is theirs, the defects are mine.

Not least I am grateful to Sister Frances Dominica – who as well as being the Founder of Helen House in Oxford was also the Mother Superior of her order – for the gracious foreword which says more about the writer than he deserves and more about the subject then he can adequately express.

Foreword

DYING IS A lonely business, especially in a society as sophisticated as our own. Money can buy most things. Power and influence can often alter the course of events. The skills and achievements of modern medicine have advanced beyond the wildest dreams of our forebears of two or three generations ago. But there comes a time for each of us when death will have its way. No other human being can travel all the way with us, but most of us will long for someone to "draw alongside", to use Sydney Callaghan's phrase, and to journey with us as far as it is possible.

Loneliness is perhaps the hardest thing to bear for those who are left behind after the death of a beloved person. Society allows us a few weeks to recover and "get back to normal" following a major bereavement. By then, we have scarcely had time to realise what has happened, let alone to adjust to the reality of living without the person we love. Religious belief may lead us to trust that the fullness of life lies beyond death, that all our longings, the yearnings of our heart, will be met in that new life. Humanitarian convictions may lead us to believe that death had brought an end to suffering for the beloved. So we may well rejoice with and for the one who has gone before us, but that does not remove from us the agonising sense of aloneness we experience, an aloneness so terrible that life itself seems pointless and death seems the better option. In this age of experts, friends, neighbours and even relatives may well consider themselves totally inadequate to the task of drawing alongside the bereaved. After all, they may reason, we don't have the skills or the experience of those whose chosen profession it is to counsel the bereaved.

Dying or bereaved, one of our greatest needs is for someone who will draw alongside and journey with us as far as may be. Which of us does not feel inadequate to such a task? (Indeed, all sorts of danger signals should flash if we feel we've got it all in the bag, we know it all, and can, all by ourselves, perform the necessary magic or miracle.)

Yet there is a sense in which each of us is qualified to be the person who will bring companionship and healing, in the deepest sense of the word, to a dying or bereaved person. Our greatest qualification lies in our common humanity, with all the inherent hopes and fears, strengths and weaknesses, frailty and glory that membership of the human race entails. So those who think they know all the tricks of the trade already need not waste their time on these chapters. But those who do read this book will be helped to believe that they do possess the necessary qualifications to bridge the gulf of loneliness, even if only a little, between themselves and those who grieve and, in consequence, between those who grieve and the world around them.

Many years ago, Sydney rolled up his sleeves and made it clear that his kind of ministry was the kind where he was prepared not only to get his hands dirty but to be in the muck right up to the eyebrows. So he writes from a rich fund of experience, weaving together practical common sense, unsentimental compassion and his own deep, lived-out faith. Through it all run the threads of honesty, humour and humility, qualities he greatly values in others. He shows us how body, mind and spirit are not separate, but together constitute a unique being. "There is only one of you in all the world. When you were created the mould was broken." These are words I shall not easily forget.

With Sydney we may feel outrage when we encounter the evasive techniques employed by many when brought face to face with death or grief. With him we may cringe when we hear ourselves or others using the clichés, the banalities or the pious platitudes which trip so readily off the tongue and which are more likely to hurt than help those on the receiving end.

Death is a universal experience. Profound grief is something most of us will experience at some time in our lives. Unless we choose to live in a hermetically sealed cocoon, closed off from the rest of humanity, each one of us will from time to time find ourselves in a place where we have the choice of drawing alongside someone who is dying or someone who is bereaved – or not. This book helps its reader to believe that the drawing alongside is not the preserve of the specialist; rather it is within the compass of us all. We need each other, just as we are, underneath all the trappings and counterfeit of false sophistication. We have the potential to journey together, all the while respecting that God-shaped space in each of us which no one else can, or should attempt to fill. So journeying, in company with death and with life, we realise that even while we experience pain so also we experience privilege. In the midst of it all we know, in the deepest part of ourselves, that the ground on which we tread on this journey is holy ground.

Mother Frances Dominica, Mother Superior General
Founder of Helen House, Oxford

Part One

*Stages of Grief:
milestones on the journey*

Good Grief

"MY GOD", HE SAID. "What a title!" How could anybody in his right mind suggest that grief could be anything but bad? Clearly this is the prattling of a priest who knows nothing about it at first hand or somebody trying to cash in on the latest craze in the caring professions – the care of the terminally ill. The next thing will be a theology of thanathalogy – an in depth study of inter-personal encounters with metaphysical phenomena. If this book turns out to be that, its writing will be a waste of time. Rather, I hope it is a practical response to those who have to encounter loss in its many facets, and a personal guide-book for the *via dolorosa* which all of us have to travel.

It does not purport to be a probing analysis of the many elements involved in the loss experience – all of which have been probed with professional skill and clinical expertise by many others – but rather a setting down of the content of lectures given to a wide variety of people who have asked for them in a more permanent form. It is not assumed for one moment that what is written has not been spelled out more ably by others elsewhere. It merely sets out to articulate the way many ordinary people have felt when travelling in 'the valley of the shadow of death'. Possibly because it draws for its insights on the experience of a wide variety of men and women it may speak to other ordinary people in a way which they will find helpful.

That is the hope which is behind it; along with the allied aim of providing some guidelines for students, both medical and theological, doctors and paramedics, nurses, both general and specialist, who want to know how they can more effectively draw alongside the suffering and bereaved without being overcome by the pain or threatened by the taboos. If for any sufferer it eases the pain, or for any carer makes the burden easier to bear, its writing will not have been in vain.

Because it draws on the experience of ordinary people and is written by one such, the result may be pedestrian rather than profound. Therein could lie part of its value. Abraham Lincoln said, "God must love the common people because he made so many of them." The learned and intellectual may look elsewhere for solace and insight. If everyday people find them in this book, it will be in a good tradition, in that it was said of the great Teacher that "the common people heard him gladly".

What I have written is part of shared experiences and there has therefore had to be respect for the privacy of other people's lives, and the avoidance of any breach of confidentiality. What has been incorporated has been done with permission. At no time has trust been betrayed or incidents written about without consent. Thus some of the most profound experiences have not been set down, in part because "the highest cannot be spoken", and partly because to have done so would have been crassly insensitive and totally uncaring. Some things must for ever remain secret. To reveal them would be an act of betrayal.

To acknowledge all of this may provide some sort of justification for the writing of this book but it does not answer the contention with which it begins. How can grief be anything but bad? How could it ever be good? That for many of us it is bad, is a fact of life. That for some it has been transformed into something good, is a fact of experience. What we are setting out to do, in company with others, is to look openly at both sets of realities.

Join us on the journey, and if you leave us en route it will not be held against you. Maybe some day you will take up the journey again. Be assured in the meantime that what is said is not spoken by one who thinks he has arrived, but by one who journeys on, striving, seeking, searching still, grateful in the meantime for sustaining resources along the way.

Setting the scene

JOSEPH PARKER, ONE time minister of the City Temple in London, used to say: "Where two or three are gathered together there is always one with a broken heart". If that appears exaggerated it does identify a truth, namely that sorrow is much more widespread than is recognised. Sorrow is a universal experience.

Each one of us encounters loss. It appears in different guises right through our lives: the child's first experience of the death of a special pet or the loss of a favourite doll; the adolescent coping with a broken heart on the break-up of the first love affair; the broken marriage, or the loss of a baby (through miscarriage or at birth), the former more common today, the latter less frequent but no less poignant. There are other 'deaths'. The loss experienced in unemployment, made worse by the notion that it can be compensated for by cash – no money can take the place of a job giving satisfaction and significance, or pay for the robbed dignity of personhood. The loss felt in major surgery or a protracted debilitating illness. The mistakenly perceived loss of femininity in a mastectomy or of sexuality in a hysterectomy or colostomy. The loss encountered in redundancy where again financial considerations are reckoned to compensate for no longer enjoying the status of position and the perks along with it.

One of the few criticisms of this section in the first edition came from a bereft mother who wrote in great anger that there was some sort of comparison between the death of her child and the loss of a pet. Of course there isn't. No two situations are ever comparable and that is not implied. Rather it is an attempt to recognise the diversity of 'deaths' people experience and the personal poignancy felt.

Another spoke of the loss of innocence experienced by the sexually abused child who has implanted the seed for potential flawed relationships in later life. Interestingly enough the opportunity to explode caused by the writer's negligence may well have been therapeutic, for the critics who reacted in a natural way were looking for a scapegoat on which to focus their anger.

It is, however, the loss in bereavement which is hardest to bear. This may be partly because so little preparation is given to it, unlike most of the major events of life. Our social structure provides antenatal care, advice to parents, pre-school groups, 'freshers' inductions to colleges and universities, initiation courses in industry and commerce, marriage preparation courses, and many other initiatives taken to equip people for life's varied experiences. But little or nothing is done about preparation for death, save by those in the religious realm, some of whom maintain that all of life is just such a process.

Perhaps this is because death is such a taboo subject, reminding us of our personal vulnerability. Twentieth-century man does not like to be reminded of his innate frailty, perhaps because death is so final and what lies beyond so unknown and unknowable. Humanity which has 'come of age' finds it hard to admit that there is so much still that we do not know, so much yet to be explored. Instead of being excited by this we are intimidated.

It is only in comparatively recent times that there has emerged a willingness by professionals in medicine and other caring disciplines to examine what is happening to both the patient and the carer in the process of dying, and to equip them for the process, emotionally as well as in other ways. In some spheres it is being resisted as having no relevance, or being outside the scope of professional responsibility. Could it be that on occasions it cuts too close to the bone, leaving us painfully aware of our common humanity when our vocation and professional codes conspire to set us apart? Being emotionally stripped naked – as the loss event has a habit of doing to all involved in it – is potentially a searing and shattering experience. It is understandable why most of us want to avoid it if at all possible. Illusions are shattered, scars are revealed and hidden things are made visible. Some cannot live with such nakedness. Some cannot take the sight of it. Some try to clothe themselves as speedily as possible, while others run away from it altogether.

For those who are prepared to grapple with their grief there is rich reward as well as much pain. The pearl may start in the oyster as a piece of grit, an irritant, but in the process of time it becomes, if not rejected, a thing of much beauty and great value. It is hard to see how this could happen to us. For those who have a mind and a will for it to do so – it can.

There is only one of you

ONE OF THE difficulties in dealing with anything related to human experience is caused by no two people being exactly alike. There is so much which we have in common that we are inclined to imagine that everybody is the same. Everybody is not. That which has meaning for one person may have none for another. Something of immense significance for one will mean little or nothing to another. The basic axiom is that each person is an individual and as such a unique entity. This must never be forgotten in our attempts at self-awareness or in our dealings with others. There is only one of you in all the world. When you were created the mould was broken.

All this is both good news and bad news. The good news is that because you are unique there is a contribution which you and you alone can make to the world we inhabit. Others may take your place or do your job – in that sense we are all totally dispensable – but nobody else can be 'you' and you are irreplaceable. That should enable you to walk with your head high, giving you a sense of worth and dignity. The input you make to life cannot be made by anybody else but you. It may not be world-shattering, or alter the course of history either personally or nationally, but you cannot be replaced.

The bad news, however, which goes along with

this, is that consequently every experience you have is totally on your own. Others may have shared a similar experience, had the same illness, been affected by common symptoms, but ultimately it is you and you alone who walk that road. The realisation that others have passed that way can be consoling and helpful at times, but the person who says "I know exactly how you feel" is repeating a nonsense. However well-intentioned the sentiments behind the statement, it is not true. He or she cannot know how you feel because he or she is not you. On a human level you walk alone. That is why it can be so intolerable. That is why it can all feel so lonesome. The sense of isolation is unbearable. We wonder if we can face any more of it.

All of this has a bearing on our theme. It must be honestly recognised that no book, no lecture, no exposition can completely identify with where each one is. How could it? However, what we can do is to look at the road and point out different milestones. If we do not observe them or have missed them, that is no reason to doubt their existence, for so many have observed them that they cannot all be mistaken, What is here intended is that in drawing attention to them, some travellers at least may recognise that they are not totally alone on their journey. Others have travelled the same road and arrived at journey's end without falling apart. This 'guide' is offered, not with the suggestion that it is the only way, for there are as many ways as there are individuals, but in the hope that some at least may find that it helps them to have an idea what to expect in the grief process, and how to deal with it.

"It couldn't happen to me"

ONE OF LIFE'S greatest delusions is summed up in the phrase: "It couldn't happen to me". It can, and it does.

We imagine it is only extraordinary people whose husbands leave them, who become terminally ill or who have a child killed in an accident. Sadly, but realistically, all these things can and do happen to ordinary people also. When events such as these do occur the reaction is often: "I simply cannot take it in. I cannot believe it has happened to me. Maybe I will wake up and discover it has all just been a bad dream. It has not really happened." Despite the evidence, we continue to cherish the thought – if it does happen it will not be to me. To others – yes, but to me – no.

This reaction can be interpreted as some form of defence mechanism. If we were always to think of every contingency, life could become impossible. It would be foolish to go out because of the possibility of an accident. It would be unwise to form relationships because of the liability of getting hurt. It would even be dangerous to go to bed at night, for the statistical fact is that more people die in bed than anywhere else. Why risk going to bed!

Flippancy apart, there are risks abounding for all of us every day. To spend too much time dwelling on them would be as unwise as it would be unhealthy. It would indeed be morbid. We would rapidly become melancholic. Nevertheless, never to contemplate life's uncertainties is unrealistic. We all share vulnerability because we all share humanity. We all live with life's liabilities as well as its possibilities.

To recognise the potential for distress and disaster facing all of us is solid worldly wisdom – it means that, if and when the dark days come, there is some preparedness to meet them. We cannot be equipped for every eventuality but we can at least be prepared for the possibility of disaster and so not totally at a loss for a rational response.

An old Scottish crofter who was dying was visited by some people who felt they should speak to him about his impending end. They found him unmoved and unimpressed by their strictures. He did not seem to make any visible response to their counsel. Finally they asked him if he did not realise he was at the end of his days. He would need to be prepared. He quietly responded that he "hadna' waited till the storm had come to thatch his house".

A disaster is not the best situation in which to produce contingency plans. It is before it takes place that we do well to think what we might do if it should happen. If it never takes place, so much the better. If it does, we are not taken unawares. There are procedures we can begin to follow. The guidance and instructions given by air crews when we take flight may seem somewhat unnecessary and mildly off-putting. Very seldom are they required to be put into operation.They are now looked on as part of the flight, and accepted as such. They have also proved for some, when a disaster has struck, to be that which enabled them to deal with it. 'Being prepared' does not produce the disaster or prevent it. But often it has minimised the effects. The flight instructions are a salutary reminder for all of life's eventualities, on all its journeys.

"It hasn't happened to me"

A COMMON REACTION to sorrow or loss is the stance expressed in the words: "It hasn't happened to me". The classic interpretation of this is called the 'denial syndrome'. The event is so disturbing or distressing that the person to whom it has happened denies altogether that it has taken place. He or she neither wishes to nor can take it in, so it is rejected. He escapes from the unpleasant by saying that it has not occurred.

The mechanism is understandable. Life throws up some terrible events. They defy reason. They are an affront to justice. They do not make any sort of sense. The human mind cannot encompass them; so it blocks them out by denial. That this happens we all know, having sometimes fallen prey to it ourselves and seeing it in others more often. (There is a funny quirk in human nature that makes us more able to spot failings in others than in ourselves, so this behaviour is always something which is done by others but never by us!)

Much is made of this behaviour in dealing with grief. It is right to recognise it. Undoubtedly it is a reaction of rejection with some. But could there not be another interpretation? Because some things are so distressing – potentially mind-blowing – nature takes a hand, gently anaesthetising us or sedating us. This is to give us time to begin to accommodate what has happened. The full impact could be so overpowering we could not take it in. A deadening of the acute reactions is brought about by a built-in sedative, the dosage quantified and given by nature itself. With consummate skill, without leaving nasty side-effects or creating an addiction, she does her work.

The reaction of disbelief and incredulity should not necessarily be seen as a handicap. In the whole process it can be something of a bonus, giving time and creating space to enable the event to sink in.

The medical profession is often wont to respond to traumatic events by providing man-made ingredients to alleviate them and their after-effects. There may be occasions when this is the most caring and professional thing to do. What is being argued here is that it is not always necessary. Sometimes it may have harmful long-term side-effects. It may deaden the immediate pain but prolong the grief by repressing it rather than grappling with it. In far too many Western cultures, doctors are responding to patients' demands. When a death takes place the doctor is automatically expected to write out a death certificate and prescribe medication for the bereaved. The former is a legal necessity, the latter can so often be a consumer's expectation which goes unquestioned.

The medical profession's response to this kind of implied criticism is that patients expect to be treated in this way, sometimes demanding it with the threat of changing doctors if they do not receive it. There is some truth in this, and evidence that it does happen. What is equally true is that short-term gratification can create longer-term problems. The more effective role of the doctor may be to refrain from prescribing, explaining why, indicating also his or her availability to follow up the loss with continued personal interest and a greater in-depth support. If adequate support is not available from him personally, he can call upon colleagues in other disciplines in the caring agencies to be his allies, available to the patient's needs in coping with loss. In an age when there has been a development not only of self-help groups but also of trained people with the appropriate skills and expertise, this could be a way of reducing the nation's drug bill, and a more creative use of the doctor's time.

"It shouldn't have happened to me"

ONE OF THE components of response to grief that is not always fully recognised or freely allowed for is anger. In Western Europe it is implied that 'nice people' do not get angry. Religious people are not supposed to know anything about it either. Religion often implies that some benign spirit wills everything for our good and that therefore whatever comes along should be accepted with stoic equanimity. To feel aggrieved and express it, is not only unchristian but uncivilised also! Such behaviour is 'unbecoming to an officer and a gentleman' or to a lady!

This attitude may appear very commendable but it is questionable whether it is either a healthy or a natural response. In the long run it is at variance with both nature and Christian behaviour. Let it therefore be conceded – anger is a basic instinct. It will manifest itself in any of us when things go wrong or do not turn out as we expect. Open recognition of the fact prevents it from being driven underground, only to look for other outlets with potential for damage to body, mind and spirit.

Loss is felt by us as an offence against our personhood. We resent it. We are angry about it. We feel aggrieved. Our sense of grievance looks for an outlet. If it does not find it in one way it will find it in another.

Sometimes anger is turned in on the self. This explains, in part, the risk of suicide or attempted suicide (both of which can be expressions of violence self-inflicted) when a bereavement has occurred. The person left behind feels angry about what has taken place so he damages himself or herself, almost to even up the score. If anger does not express itself in forms as extreme as that, it can certainly have other effects on the health of people left behind.

A senior nursing officer spoke with some relief about a new-found explanation for the periods of sick leave which she had had to take after her mother's death, but for which there was no satisfactory medical explanation. The illness was real, the symptoms were authentic, but no reason could be found for them. Such a thing had never happened to her before. She had never been absent for a day's sick leave in all her career. When she started to explore the relationship between anger and health she began to piece together bits of the human jigsaw puzzle. She had always been the coping daughter who had to do everything. When her mother died her brothers were helpless, so again she had to make all the arrangements. Her statutory permitted three days of compassionate leave were fully occupied with dealing with all that had to be done. Her subsequent return to duty was followed some time later by an undiagnosed illness. In speaking of her discovery of the anger/illness tie-up she admitted that she saw, for the first time, a rational explanation for what had happened. It all began to make sense. She had been angry inwardly. She had not been given time to grieve. Nature therefore decided obligingly to make time to enable her to do so. It would have been so much better for her self-esteem if her anger had not needed to find expression in the way it did.

In these days of evaluating cost-effectiveness in the caring agencies, it is suggested that there could be some merit in allowing staff on compassionate leave to stay away till they feel able to come back, rather than impose a blanket rule which implies that we can all get our act together three days after a personal or domestic tragedy. Maybe some can do this, and even find a healing in the return to work. Others do not. Such people may well in the long run put their own and others' health at risk through loss of efficiency and a resultant inability to cope with the demands of their job. If some cynics say such an arrangement would not work, then let us evaluate whether our present approach always works in the best interests of all concerned.

Anger felt by the bereaved may be an extension of the anger felt by the dying person in terminal illnesses. Such anger is often turned on those around about, with its greatest intensity felt by those nearest. The sufferer is feeling angry about what is happening to him, especially as so often he is kept in the dark about his condition and its prognosis. Able to see for himself that he does not appear to be getting better he resents the half-truths: "You're doing fine" (but they didn't tell you they couldn't get all the cancer removed); "You're looking a lot better" (but it is only a short-term remission of the condition); "You're coming on nicely" (but I thought it better not to mention that the condition is terminal). He is not stupid, and is irritated by being treated as mentally inadequate as well as physically ill. "Why can't people come clean and be honest with me?" he feels. Because they do not – all in his interest, is their defence – mental turmoil is added to his bodily pain. No wonder there is anger. It would be strange if there were not.

The anger is not often expressed to the doctor, the nurse or the priest; they may be needed some time, so better not risk alienating them. It does manifest itself most viciously against those who are closest. Here again is the paradox that we hurt most deeply the ones we love the most. Understanding the psychology of what is happening will help the family circle and relieve some of the pain. It is as though the sufferer is hitting out, is crying out. He knows something is happening to him – but what, he is not sure. He is coping with uncertainty and sometimes living with fear. He wants to be sure that, for all the unpleasant and unattractive (at times) expressions of his disability, he is still wanted, loved and dear; so he strikes out at those close to him, pushing them like mad, because he needs to know that despite what pain is doing to his body and his personality he still has a place in their lives. He is saying: "If you can't take it, then it's all over, or it might as well be, since even you have given up."

There are few nurses who have not had the experience of visiting a dying patient at home to find him cheerful and in good form, but being shown another picture when the partner accompanies the nurse to the car. As the door is about to be closed the wife breaks down: "Nurse, I can't take any more of this. He is simply terrible. No matter what I do, it is wrong. The children are getting on his nerves. He's great with you. He thinks you are wonderful. He's so chatty and cheerful with everybody else. With me it is different. He's a different person. It's almost a personality change. It's all so unfair, especially when I am doing all I can. He doesn't seem to be able to see what it is all doing to me. I've had more than I can take." Skilled is the nurse who listens without interruption and, when the storm has died down, the sobbing ceased, is able to reassure the wife that in its own zany way the patient's behaviour is the greatest compliment he can pay her. He is saying: "Deep down I want to feel that you can take it and will see me through. I believe you can. I realise I'm being horrible but I can't help it, for I feel so shattered and lost. I can't let myself go with the others, but with you I can. I can see the pain in your eyes. I recognise the fatigue. I know you are doing all you can, but please, please don't go away." Being able to be totally himself, stripped of all the reserves and defences, is the most profound compliment a person can pay in any relationship, albeit one hell of a difficult one to cope with at the time.

Sometimes the anger is turned on God. Who

better to blame than him – after all isn't he supposed to be responsible for the whole set-up? People who have no formal religious beliefs find it useful to 'have a go' at God – it all simply confirms what they have always known. If he exists at all, he isn't particularly caring. If he was he wouldn't allow any of the terrible things that happened, to happen. If he is in charge of things, as religious people say he is, he is a 'right old so-and-so' and one has every right to feel angry with him.

For the person who has some formal faith, suffering can pose an even greater problem. God is always regarded as good and kind, but if he is, he should not allow what has happened to me or mine to take place. When it does, there is a sense of outrage but also a feeling of guilt about being angry with him. One is not supposed to be angry with God. And yet, why not?

A deeply committed Christian who was also a very caring nurse told how shocked she was by a family in her care who belonged to the church of which she was a member.They were held in high esteem because of their profession of faith. They were known for their great piety and intense devotion. So she was somewhat shattered when she witnessed their reaction to impending death, when their defences were down. She found it hard to reconcile what they had always purported to be with how they actually were. In the crisis they appeared to undergo a personality change. Some became blasphemous and profane. What had happened to their faith? Had it all been a sham? It was difficult not to feel let down, and even not to question the reality of her own beliefs. She was reassured when she was helped to understand that the patient was angry, and angry with God. It was coming out in this way, a verbal shaking of the fist at the Almighty. If she did not understand it, he certainly did. "He knows our frame; he remembers that we are dust" (Psalm 103:14). He does not hold it against us that we are aggrieved. Indeed, he recognises what we should also, namely that we only tend to become intensely angry with those with whom we have some sort of involvement. Our expression of bitterness to God about what is going on is an indication of a relationship, albeit it is strained at that moment. He understands us. No matter how much abuse we pile on him, he still cares. He will never give up doing that. The child who is angry with his father or mother may viciously strike out at them but will never forfeit the love of the genuine parent because he or she will always go on loving. "If you then, who are evil, know how to give good gifts to your children, how much more will your Father who is in heaven . . ." (Matthew 7:11).

Anger is our natural response when there is loss, pain, hurt or suffering. It is not wrong to feel it. It is not out of order to express it. The wise and supportive carer and friend will make space to allow for its expression, remains unshocked at its manifestation and shows there is still acceptance by those to whom it is expressed, because they too have come to recognise the dormant volcano in us all.

"Why has it happened to me?"

THE COMING OF anything unpleasant to any of us invariably produces a reaction of: "Why me?" It seldom occurs to us to ask: "Why not me?", or to question "why me?" if what takes place is a thing of pleasure or delight. From among the smouldering ashes of anger or the passionate flames of rage there always emerges the query, "Why?"

Perhaps the first thing to realise is that it is much more a cry from the heart than an intellectual query. We deal with it mistakenly if we treat it as the latter. It is not that there is no place for the philosophical query – there is, but not then and there. The agonising cry of the broken-hearted is not helped by the language of cold logic. To respond in that way would be as insensitive and unwise as debating the relative merits of private health care and the National Health Service at a major road accident! A speedy intervention to ease the pain and to stifle the risk of further damage is what is required. The caring response is to draw alongside and offer the most appropriate aid to lessen the immediate distress. It is pain killers that are required, not philosophers!

Realistically it must be conceded that at any rate there are some questions to which there are no totally satisfactory answers here and now. We are finite beings trying to understand infinite reality. There are things which are beyond our understanding. The apostle Paul, with his deep personal faith, nevertheless acknowledges: "Now I know in part; then I shall understand fully, even as I have been fully understood" (1 Corinthians. 13:12). Our knowledge here is partial. We shall only fully understand later on.

It is this which makes the know-all, especially of the religious variety, so out of place at a time of distress. He is not only out of place but often something of a menace – a danger to himself and a danger to others. The danger for him is that he is on very shaky theological ground, believing himself to know what cannot be known. The danger to others is that in the time of their vulnerability he makes them feel guilty about asking *why*. Further, they mistake his arrogance for assurance. In their uncertainties, impressed by his certainty, they clasp to their breasts what he is saying, only to be left with a greater ache within when they find that if it all makes sense to him it does not to them. Their self-confidence, already at a low ebb, takes another blow, leading to an even greater despair.

None of this is to imply that there is no place for seeking answers to the problem of pain. Rather is it the recognition that there is "a time to speak and a time to keep silent." The time to speak is certainly not when the cry comes from the heart rather than the mind. Let heart speak to heart, in language without words, that meets the need at the deep level. At the time of deepest need there is no answer to the 'why' from within. It is unkind and dishonest to imply that there is.

What answer is there to the 'why' from a broken-hearted mother nursing her cot-death baby? Few can understand what she feels – and certainly no man can fully do so. He has never carried a baby as part of his body for nine months, or had a child feed from his breasts. Men may start babies. They do not grow them within as "bone of our bone, flesh of our flesh" in the way a woman does. While a man can try to enter into how she feels he cannot do so other than intellectually or with insight or imagination – never experientially. It is beyond his range of being.

What satisfactory answer is there to the shattered parents of a bright-eyed, happy little boy electrocuted while trying to be helpful by bringing a table lamp from the veranda, because it had started to rain? Do we mouth platitudes to add to their pain and so reveal the banality of our thinking?

What can we say when a delightfully vivacious young colleague dies, having fought against cancer for five years with yearly surgical encounters and skirmishes with radiotherapy and chemotherapy, leaving behind a widow and two children under three years of age? Do we meekly say: "One day we will understand"? Do we not also say through our tears: "Why?", "Why?", "Why?" If we don't, we are less than human and we will certainly never be able to help those who do.

One of the most moving passages in the Passion narrative in the Gospels is the point in the crucifixion where Jesus cries out: "My God, my God, why have you forsaken me?" It has been implied that it was an almost involuntary cry, coming from deep down in the subconscious, part of a childhood recollection of the Psalms in which his early days were nurtured. (A parallel has been drawn with the reflection of the elderly confused who can be vague about yesterday's events although recalling with clarity the poems they learned as children in their early days at school.) Others have tried to dismiss it as being a human state of mild confusion stemming from the effects of his tortuous pain – it was not how he felt at all; how could the divine in him feel deserted? Whatever the theological explanation, the statement has a deep pastoral content. Jesus clearly felt deserted. He had an overpowering feeling of being alone. That was for real. Doubtless the Pauline insight is correct that "God was in Christ reconciling the world to himself" (2 Corinthians 5:19); but for Jesus at that moment he felt totally alone, utterly deserted, and so expressed his cry of dereliction. That he did so, brings its own consolations to others undergoing their own calvaries. At least they can feel that he would understand. Despite the well-intentioned words of friends – "I understand" – there remains the haunting knowledge that no one can possibly do so unless he or she has also been at the point of utter dereliction, expressed in such a despairing cry.

Jesus in his anguish cried: "My God, why?" He would not condemn us for doing the same. Disregard those who say: "You shouldn't ask why", by reminding them that Jesus did. Desist from the guilty feeling for doing so. Perhaps as we try to catch our breath between our tears and sobs, if we pause long enough and listen in the quiet, we will hear a voice assure us in the age-old promise: "When you pass through the waters I will be with you" (Isaiah 43:2). God does not say "if" you do, but "when". Despite all our feelings to the contrary, he is closer than breathing and nearer than hands or feet.

What are we affirming here? Surely this – on the one hand the honest acknowledgement of the unanswerable "why" arising from the broken heart and the bruised spirit; and on the other, the quiet statement of personal conviction that despite all appearances to the contrary our heavenly Father does not desert his children in their hour of need. It is with this tension between healthy agnosticism and heartfelt assurance, that the Christian lives. It has been aptly expressed by John Greenleaf Whittier, the American Quaker poet:

> Here in the maddening maze of things,
> When tossed by storm and flood,
> To one fixed ground my spirit clings,
> I know that God is good.
>
> I know not what the future hath
> Of marvel or surprise,

Assured alone that life or death,
His mercy underlies.

I know not where his islands lift
Their fronded palms in the air,
I only know I cannot drift
Beyond his love and care.

That seems to say it all. There is so much I do not know; but the One I do know will see me through.

Some there are who will feel unable to accept this as a reality. They only know the cry of agonising despair. They have not heard any reassuring voice. They only know the darkness. For and to them, we can only say: "We sincerely understand what you feel and say, having said it ourselves. If you cannot relate to the note of reassurance which has seen us through our own dark night of the soul, do not be dismissive of it altogether or feel that our sharing it is a manifestation of some sort of patronising spirituality. It is not intended to be. We can only assure you that for us it is authentic. We promise that at a human level we will be around and stay alongside of you until a new day dawns for you and the shadows flee away. If it never happens, we will still try to hang around as long as you need us."

What more can we promise than that?

"I feel sad that it has happened to me"

THERE IS AN amazing unwillingness in some societies to allow for sadness. While it may be acknowledged, it is thought to be unseemly to express it publicly. There is embarrassment even when it is expressed privately. In the Anglo-Saxon tradition it just isn't done. In the Calvinist Puritan tradition there is a stoicism which sees any show of feelings as out of place. This is all rather strange, and at variance with the natural responses of most ordinary people elsewhere. It may be that in some cultures people do go overboard on grief, hence the Western reaction. But the denial of sadness and any expression of it is both unreal and unhealthy. Sadness is a natural reaction to grief and loss. To express it is to show ourselves as part of the human family. How it will manifest itself will tend to vary from person to person and from culture to culture, but it is important to recognise that it has a place in the journey from disintegration to integration.

Most of us can remember a childhood experience of loss, be it either temporary or permanent. We recall the sadness when a favourite doll was left behind somewhere and thought to be gone forever. Despite the fact that it had only one eye and the leg was hanging off, you were inconsolable till it was found to be safe and well. There were many others, as your father reminded you, but it did not stop you sobbing out: "But they are not the same. I want my special dolly." The little pup who used to sleep at the end of your bed, who went everywhere with you, who got run over by a car, left you so upset that you could not eat your food for days.

These experiences of pain and loss left an impression. You can still feel something of the anguish of them even after all these years. They are seen in another perspective now. Other pains and heartaches have superseded the early inklings of sadness. You may possibly make light of your childishness now. But the intuition of the child was right. Grief must find an outlet. If it does not do so, it can cause trouble later on.

If we can be so shattered by the loss of some toy or some animal companion as a child, is it not to be expected that we will feel a little distress when a partner or loved one dies? It would be very strange if we did not. Some sensitive instinct would have gone from our lives. Socially programmed responses would have taken over. Feelings would have died. Sorrow is the natural response to loss. We should not be afraid to express it, nor be at a loss how to deal with it in others. Later we will look at some of the classic everyday expressions of it. It is enough for now to be aware of it and not to be surprised by either sorrow or joy.

Reference has already been made to the responses of children to the loss of a pet or plaything. Such an experience can be very traumatic. Even more so can be the long-term illness or death of a brother, sister or parent. More sensitive techniques have been developed in recent years in helping children with their grieving. It has sometimes been imagined that, because their feelings are not as developed as the adults' – or so it used to be thought – their pain is less. There need be no catering for them – "They are only children," it was said. This is wrong. They too have their sense of loss. They must not only be allowed to express it in their own way, but encouraged to do so as well as sharing in the whole grief experience. In that way we help to rid them of some of our taboos and give them the more excellent way of dealing with one of life's universal statistics.

"I feel bad that it has happened to me"

THE WORD 'BAD' has a number of different connotations, one of which at least has a moral dimension. Allied to that is a sense of achievement – or self-righteousness – about having done the right thing, or a feeling of guilt about wrong things done or good things left undone. So often is heard the cry: "Why did I …?" or more frequently: "Why didn't I …?" The bereaved carry burdens of regret and remorse – some without any real reason for doing so, and others quite rightly living with recollections of wrongs done which cannot be undone, or things which should have been done which could have put matters right.

The burden is increased for some people by the thought that what has happened is some sort of judgment. "Am I being punished for something, padre?" "Maybe I'm being got at for all the wrong things I've done." These or similar sentiments are expressions of guilt feelings and as such can be expected, with greater intensity in some people than in others.

Guilt is not always necessarily a bad thing. Not all its end results are negative. There is in this century the idea that when man comes of age he will no longer feel this way. "For the mature adult there is no such thing as guilt." It is regarded as a by-product of religious notions that our society has outgrown. Maybe we have. Could that in part be the explanation for some of the antisocial behaviour which disrupts communities and breaks down personal and family relationships? If there is no component of culpability there is frequently no sense of responsibility. "It does not matter what I do," so the argument runs. "I am a free agent. If others get hurt because of my activities that's just their hard luck. It's no skin off my nose."

On the other hand, the possibility of feeling guilty can be a deterrent, and for some of us it is as well that something of that nature exists! It may not be the loftiest of ideals. Virtue must always be its own reward. To realise that some things are not worth getting caught up in because of the price to be paid afterwards is the sort of deterrent in which the guilt factor can play a part. It is perhaps well for some that a preventative 'medicine' acts as a possible antidote.

It is useful to recognise all of this, but equally useful to realise that there is a guilt which is negative and can be totally destructive. From it little or no good comes. It can express itself in two very different forms.

There is the possibility of becoming obsessed with guilt. The patient or client gets hooked on the memory of things done or left undone. He talks incessantly along the lines of: "Why did I?" or: "Why didn't I?" On and on it goes. Sometimes it is accompanied by walking up and down without stopping, or a continuous sobbing which cannot be stifled, the question interposed with a recurring frequency. Any reasoned response from the would-be counsellor or friend falls on deaf ears. The condition has become what is described as 'pathological'. It needs skilled psychiatric attention, partly because of the intensity of the condition and partly because it may be so deep-seated as to be a symptom of a deeper problem rather than the problem itself. There is a danger here of involving the amateur psychologist, clerical or lay, who proffers pious platitudes or self-help remedies! True, the Christian is helped and healed by the realisation of the truth that "the blood of Jesus, God's Son, cleanses from all sin (1 John 1:7), but to glibly bandy about the panacea may not be exactly what that person needs at that particular time. Indeed, it could make things worse, in that if no 'healing' comes to the 'guilty soul', he may begin to talk about the possibility of his having committed the unpardonable sin. That can lead into both a psychological and a theological minefield. This note of caution needs to be sounded, since in the loss experience we are particularly vulnerable. Bereaved people require to be handled with both care and sensitivity as well as professional skill. Dabblers beware!

The other possible reaction is a moving into a fantasy world. The sense of guilt is so overpowering that the only way to cope is by seeing the situation as other than it actually was. Many of us have encountered couples whose marriages have been a hell on earth, who had frequently talked of divorce, even going to the length of obtaining legal advice – unknown to each other but spoken of to their friends. Suddenly one of the partners dies, leaving the other heart-broken. Months later she speaks of how much she misses him. "I can't live without him. We never had a cross word with each other. We went everywhere together ..." She goes on and on in such vein until the hearer wonders whether he has made a mistake and got things all wrong! He hasn't. It is that the wife has moved into a fantasy world of make-believe. She cannot cope with the recollection of the reality and her contribution to its hellishness, so she tells herself – and everybody else – that it was wonderful. In that way the unpalatable becomes more acceptable and the pain of the recollection becomes more bearable. Friends who are trying to help in this kind of situation should be warned – whatever you do, do not feel you have some responsibility to put the record straight. You will neither help her or keep her friendship if you do. Time may enable her to recall more clearly or accurately what was the true state of affairs. In the meantime be a good listener. You may find that, before her record becomes a golden disc, she has tired of it somewhat and changed to a new tune! You will grow weary with it, but you may well have helped her along the road to reality.

"But it has happened to me"

MATURITY COMES IN life to those who have learned to accept. If that is so, it is clear that some have never reached maturity. They cannot come to terms with what has happened. The brokenness cannot be accepted. They torment themselves with what might have been, but wasn't, They tear themselves apart by their unwillingness to come to terms with reality. We have grown up when we have arrived at the place of acknowledgment.

Perhaps we need to clarify that we can acknowledge something without necessarily accepting it. The difference lies in realising the different levels of illumination. An event can be intellectually processed but not necessarily emotionally so. Experience would seem to indicate a time gap between the intellectual reaction and the feeling response. A common mistake is to think it all happens at the same time. With some it may. For most it does not.

The actual event or happening forces a mental response. The mind has to react out of sheer necessity. Something has to be done about what has happened. The emotions are not so programmed. It takes time for the message to get from head to heart. We must allow for this time gap. Failure to do so can create difficulties. In the hiatus there is possible danger and considerable risk.

The danger can be seen when, with hindsight, we recall colleagues and friends who have suffered some personal blow who return to work and everyday routine. As the weeks go by we say to other friends: "How well she is doing. She is coming along fine." Then one day we hear that she is in hospital after an overdose. We are shocked, totally taken by surprise. Somebody who was so rational about things, had accepted everything so well was, it would seem, still in turmoil. We had been taken in by the appearance of acceptance. The head was saying "I'm fine", but the heart was contradicting it. We had not noticed this, partly because we wanted her to be fine and partly because the clues to her distress were so well concealed that we had not been aware of them.

The risk for someone who has suffered loss stems from vulnerability. He or she can so often do things in an emotional vacuum totally at variance with their usual reactions. This is understandable because the person is not 'at himself', as we say in the Irish idiom. It is incidentally a most apt expression because it describes the condition so perceptibly.

We have all seen this but felt powerless to stop it – the broken engagement leading to an unhelpful liaison; the job loss which precipitates a move to another country; major surgery causing an inappropriate domestic decision. The classic example is the death of a parent, bringing about the break-up of a home with disastrous results: "Let's bring Mum to live with us. She'll be lost without Dad and we have the spare room. She gets on so well with the children." It all seems such a good idea at the time, so caring, so considerate. The scene six months later is very different. Mum is getting on everybody's nerves. "Why is Granny so difficult? It used to be great when she came to see us but she's always picking on me and going on about the noise of the record player. She won't let me watch my favourite TV programme but expects us to be quiet when hers are on . . ." Everybody is getting on Mum's nerves. "I don't wish to complain, dear, but the children are getting out of hand and they can be so rude, even to you, but you don't seem to notice it!" The husband is slowly going up the walls with Mother-in-law who could be taken in small doses but is becoming more difficult to take, especially as she is always going on about giving up her home and all her belongings to come and live in a place where she knows nobody. The poor wife and mother is caught up in the middle of the aggravation. It all seems so unfair, as she was only doing it for the best. She has to cope with all this along with her own grieving for a father she dearly loved (resenting him having died, leaving Mum behind, because he would have been so much easier to have around, and then feeling guilty of even thinking like that). So much of this could have been avoided if only somebody had advised all concerned to make no significant move for at least a year after the trauma of the major upheaval.

He was a delightful little man. He lived next

door to us in an excellent residential home. The housekeeper's care and cooking was so good that we often threatened to move in there ourselves! One day he called by, ostensibly to make a phone call but principally for a chat. (The professionals call it recognising the difference between the presenting problem and the real one!) Was he happy there? asked Brenda. Not really, he said. It had all been a great mistake. He went on to say why.

He had been married for many years. They had lived in a big house with a large garden to look after. He had nursed his wife during her terminal illness. Everybody told him that when she died, the house would be too big and the garden too much for him. He should give them up. Get into something smaller. "I was foolish enough to listen to them," he admitted. "I sold the house and came to live here. It was the greatest mistake of my life" – which was possibly true, not because the care and accommodation was not excellent, for it was, but because he was not emotionally ready for the move when it took place.

He was coping with the loss of a wife, the loss of a routine, the loss of a home – each significant losses on their own, but all three were too much at the one time. Possibly to have waited a year to cope with the death of his wife, another year to recognise that it was not all that easy to manage everything on his own, and then with decreasing physical powers to have come to his own decision as to what was best – that would have been the right way; but not as it was. He wasn't 'at himself' when it all happened and it was all too much for him. Before such decisions are made, head and heart must be at one. If part of us has reached a point of acceptance and another part has not, there cannot be the unity of purpose.

It is always easy to see these things clearly when they happen to others. It is not quite so simple when we are personally involved. To illustrate this, and at the same time to encapsulate the thrust of this whole point, an example from personal experience is perhaps not out of place.

My mother died when she was eighty-six years of age. She had been happily married to a husband who had predeceased her years beforehand. She had lived on her own since then, with family support. For seven years prior to her death, increased physical disability and mental senility meant that she was a patient in a nursing home. The deterioration was distressing to behold. What had once been a woman of much beauty, physical strength and personal charm degenerated into a frail old lady whose every need required attention by others, whose speech and communication skills – even to the loss of expression in her vivacious blue eyes – no longer functioned. This process was hard to take. When the moment of death came, shared with her by the family, it was both a moment of relief and a release. It was a release for her and a relief for us. She was set free from the limitations and frustrations of a body no longer fully functioning into a sphere where limitations are transformed into liberty and frustrations into freedom. It was a relief for us as her children, relief not from a burden but from a pain.

There was no difficulty in accepting all of this conceptually. There were things to be done, a service of worship and thanksgiving to be conducted, affairs to be settled up, life to go on living. There was no difficulty in accepting the psycho-geriatric condition, as her diagnosis was described. Indeed, the encounter with all of this was an invaluable pastoral asset then and subsequently – but, and here is the big but, the acceptance of it all emotionally was another matter altogether. It is one thing to know and to be able to describe clinically the symptoms of the psycho-geriatric condition, but it is different altogether when the condition is personalised and it is one's own mother. That is harder to accept emotionally than the clinical description, no matter how well tutored one may be professionally. The words of committal can be affirmed with passion and sincere belief when we "lay to rest those who have died in the Lord", but when it is one's own mother who is the "mortal putting on immortality", then it tugs at the heart-strings. There comes the realisation, no matter how sincerely one accepts theologically all that is said, that the emotional acceptance of the chapter end which is death is harder to come by and takes longer. When eventually heart and mind are in harmony, the acceptance is full and complete. We are then free to move on.

"I feel sort of glad that it has happened to me"

To some people the idea expressed by this phrase is so unbelievable as to make it almost offensive. It could not be true that something of such hurt and distress could bring any happiness or enrichment – and yet it is a truth to which many people have borne witness. As such, it merits consideration.

To those who are in the midst of a painful period such an admission will sound empty and hollow. That is understandable and not unreasonable. All that can be asked for is a willingness to concede that it might be possible, as for some it has been. It must not be taken as a serious reflection upon either one's faith or one's character if it does not happen. For some it never does. What is being reflected here is an honest statement of a fact in human experience. From it we can learn. By it we can be challenged.

No painful experience is pleasant. Put another way – some of the darkest nights are so dreadful, it is impossible to imagine any light of any sort at the end of the tunnel. It is dark despair. "I will never be able to get over this" – words we have all heard. Many of us have used them ten, fifteen, twenty years further on, and they will sometimes confess: "I didn't think I would make it. I would not wish to live through anything like that again, but somehow now I feel a bit different about it all." The wound has healed, and healed cleanly. The scar remains and always will. The wound can be opened up again; but as the years have rolled on the scar has become incorporated into the skin-patterns and hardly discernible to the naked eye. To the keen observer, with a sharp eye, the markings of the wound are still visible, but to the casual passer-by it cannot be seen. Unless you know of it or have been told of it, you will not be aware of it. The wound has healed. All is well.

Something further can happen. From the painful experience there can come gain. Much has been written about the positive value of suffering – most of it by those who have known little of it at first hand! Let us face the fact that pain can be totally debilitating. Few in the caring professions have not seen it devastate people to a totally unrecognisable degree. It has destroyed them. Their suffering has robbed them of their dignity and self-respect. It has left them shattered and disillusioned. They have become physical and emotional wrecks. People who were once kind and good have become nasty and aggressive. As they become shadows of their former selves, what has emerged is ugly and unattractive.

Let us not sentimentalise suffering or trivialise trauma. It can create a bloody, awful mess. It often does. Equally, we affirm, it does not always do so. There are those who have said: "It was hell at the time, I would not want to live through the like of it again; but now, looking back, strange as it may be to say it, I would not have missed it for anything."

When people say something like that, especially if they strike us as being sane, normal folk, it is useful to probe a bit deeper because it is not the sort of reaction we would expect. It seems to be at such variance with what we would have imagined. When asked, such people have often replied along these lines: "I came to know myself in a new way." "I found out who my real friends were." "I discovered resources of help and strength about which I had heard but never felt to be for real." "It was almost like being born all over again." Different forms of words, reflecting a profound, sometimes almost imperceptible change, altering stances and attitudes so that life has never been quite the same since it all happened.

It would be totally dishonest to imply that such a reorientation is the sole prerogative of religious people. Some who would not profess to have any religious beliefs claim to have experienced it. At a human level, they admit it has brought changes to their lives. They are possibly less arrogant and more aware of others and their feelings. They have a greater insight into the human condition. They found that some people on whom they thought they could rely backed off and could not help them meet the needs of the hour. They also found help and consolation from the most unlikely people. Their personal and professional lives were enriched. They feel themselves to be more mature persons, more competent professionals.

Quite a number of religious people would claim that for them the suffering has brought values to their lives which were previously not there before, or which were previously dormant. That is not to say that they see suffering as God-given, to be endured and used, although some devout people would so interpret it; but rather as something which can be used by God who constantly wills the highest and best for all his children because he loves them.

Let me illustrate this again from personal experience. Passing through a period of a loss of relationship and personal disappointment I shared with my father for whom I had both a deep regard and a great affection. My father, with great feeling and sensitivity, wrote to me of his feeling of sadness for me, saying how he wished he could have taken the pain to himself and saved me from the hurt, but it was not possible. (This sentiment is often expressed by parents to their children, who view it with a certain benevolent scepticism until they themselves become parents, recognising both the privilege and the pain of parenthood. The privilege to be permitted to share in the creation and formation of another life. The pain – seeing those we love in distress and being unable to do anything about relieving it.) He went on to say that he was certain that God had not sent this hurt. Just as he would not deliberately cause pain to his children, neither would a loving heavenly Father – indeed even less so because his love is without flaw and blemish – inflict pain on any of his family. What, however, God could do was to take the distress and use it in such a way that gain could be made and enrichment achieved. He spoke of Weymouth's happy rendering of Paul's words: "the pain which God allowed to guide". He said that if I could see it in that light and take it that way, all of this God could use. In my service to God it could be of benefit and consolation to others in that they would encounter somebody who knew heartache at first hand, who understood failure and so had insight into how they might feel and be aware of where they stood.

It would be presumptuous to claim that this is what has happened or how it has been personally processed, but if insight has been gained, people helped, hurt understood, then in part it has been due to its having been seen in that way and accepted in that spirit. The opportunity to apply what was learned has perhaps done a little to see others through hard times and to be available to them till a better time comes.

What has been spoken of personally has been exemplified by others also. Doctors and nurses have testified how their views and strategies of patient care were forever altered by having been patients themselves. The view of illness is very different from the bed than from the bedside. Social workers have said that they understood mental illness only academically until they were themselves off work for six months with depression. Clergy have admitted they knew about marital problems only as case studies until it came to their own doorsteps. All have confessed that the experience was the most difficult thing they ever had to deal with, but having been through it they look back on it all as a learning experience from which they have gained so much that they would not have missed it for anything. Well, perhaps not quite as euphoric as that, but at least they were able to say, despite the sadness, the heart-break and the pain, "I'm sort of glad it happened to me."

I have indicated some milestones on the journey – but they do not necessarily have to be stopping places:
"It couldn't happen to me."
"It hasn't happened to me."
"It shouldn't have happened to me."
"Why has it happened to me?"
"I feel sad that it has happened to me."
"I feel bad that it has happened to me."
"But it has happened to me."
"I feel sort of glad that it has happened to me."

Now we look at what can be done to help either ourselves or others, when the bottom falls out of life. Again we must recognise that our individuality means that what can be helpfully significant to one may not be so for another. It will not do us any harm to have at least some ideas of the antidotes available for our grief and the resources available to help others to cope with theirs. No list can be exhaustive, no remedy fully satisfying for everybody; but to know where the remedies lie or where they can be procured is at least a helpful beginning.

Part Two

*Realities, Remedies and
Resources*

Team

EVERY TRADE OR profession has its jargon. Every discipline has its 'in' theories. The 'in' theory with the caring professions just now is the team concept. We are all being encouraged to work as a team, frequently by people whose ideas of it depend on their being captain or vice-captain! The thought of their being only a 'sub' now and then, or left off altogether never occurs to them. If that were to be suggested, the team concept would doubtless be replaced by another theory of management. Yet for all that – and it is easy to poke fun at these ideas, as we all should from time to time lest we take ourselves too seriously – there is much in this approach which is invaluable when dealing with people in distress.

It is invaluable from the helpers' viewpoint because it prevents inflated notions of one's own importance. A constant danger for those who are dealing with people at risk comes from the fact that the latter are so weak and vulnerable and the former in positions of such strength and influence. The helper can feel so strong and good. Indeed he or she may be encouraged to feel like that by the adulation of colleagues and the appreciation of his 'beneficiaries'. "She is very good at handling people," says the evaluation. "You have been a great help to me," says the client. All of this can be good for our self-esteem. It may be bad for our ego if we begin to actually believe it, forgetting that with all flattery and commendation we should sniff but not inhale!

A much more realistic approach stems from the realisation that I am not the answer to every problem or able to meet all the needs of everybody. Indeed, the facets of my personality which may be of help to one person could well be an irritant to another. When a team is operative, varieties of personal abilities and resources are available to the person in need. He or she must be our primary concern. His 'permission to write the agenda' is what matters. Our willingness to allow this to happen is a measure of our personal and professional maturity. If he or she is seen as 'my' client or patient only, it may be more an indicator of my need of him or her, rather that the other way around.

It is predictable that in some circumstances a person will relate to his helper at a very deep level. He may have no wish to relate to anybody else. That should be permitted so long as it does not develop into a fixation, which it can do unless monitored skillfully. By the same token a client may not be able to relate to his allocated support, because of some subliminal remembered or half-remembered memory creating negative 'vibes'. All involved must be big enough to allow for this. Hence the value of the team approach rather than the solo effort.

A matron in a hospice, when asked what were the qualities she looked for in her staff, replied, "Hard work, humour and humility." Hard work, because the nature of the task demanded it. There was no room for the clock-watcher. A sense of humour was required in that "you couldn't work here unless you had it." Humility was a prerequisite because there were times when the cleaner was being of greater help to the patient than the consultant, and the lady who changed the flowers of more actual support than the chaplain. All of that is profoundly true.

Being involved with grief and loss is hard work. Grief cannot be contained within the nine to five context. At all hours of the day or night it can call out for help and support. Availability is important for those in need. Their demands during the crisis can be well nigh overpowering. Regulating life in terms of job descriptions or person-hours involved, while being desirable from the helper's point of view, is a recipe for creating despair for the patient.

A sense of humour is an essential ingredient in any branch of the caring professions. The closer we work to the edge in suicide prevention or terminal care the more essential humour is. If we are to see ourselves in perspective and to help others retain theirs, we require the capacity to laugh as well as cry. There is no contradiction between laughter and tears – they are both emotional responses to out of the ordinary events, laughter the feeling of joy, tears of sorrow.

Humility, a virtue easy to speak of but harder to practise, is not a characteristic associated with many professional people. Education and training can produce a sense of achievement, bringing an attitude of attainment, which in turn produces a high degree of self-esteem. It is not easy for the person who through dint of hard work or through innate ability has gone far, to think lowly of himself. The two most arrogant types some of us meet are consultants and clerics, the former because they are treated like 'Lord God

Almighty', the latter because they think they are! This of course is not always true, in that some of the most gracious and humble people encountered have been among their number. But some of the most arrogantly offensive have also been found among their number. Their attitude may stem from their training or from their perspective on their role, but it can turn out some most unattractive specimens. Reliable defusers of professional pomposity are a personal sense of humour, or a family who bring them down to ground level every so often!

The matron was right in looking for these qualities. They are essential for any team of people working together. There is also another vital quality – honesty. This expresses itself in an openness in dealing with each other and candour in our relationships with our patients,

No team work can operate successfully unless there is trust. This does not mean that all team members have to see eye-to-eye on everything – how dull that would be! It does mean that there is a personal regard for each other and an acknowledgement of the professional skills of those from other disciplines. Any stances of superiority by any member of the team over others will minimise the team's effectiveness and undermine relationships. Each one has to be open to the other, with a willingness to accept each other, warts and all.

Important as is the need for openness amongst the team, honesty is if anything even more important between the team and those whom they serve and support.

The debate about what to tell and what not to tell terminally ill patients is one which has engaged doctors and their colleagues for a long time. There are different schools of thought with consequently varied approaches down the line. One tradition takes the view: tell the patient nothing. This is to treat the patient with scant dignity and little regard. It implies either that he had no right to know, or that he would be incapable of dealing with it if he did know. Those who support this school of thinking seem to forget that the patient is not stupid, that he is capable of picking up non-verbal communication and that he should therefore be told about his situation. They fail to appreciate the strain of uncertainty. They seem to forget that the patient has a lot of time to think for himself, that when the round is over, when the visitors have gone, he is left to his own uncertainties and memories of half-heard snatches of the bedside consultation between doctors and students (who apparently have a greater right to know, to probe and to ask questions than the patient).

Another school of thought takes the opposite view: "Tell them everything. No beating about the bush." Tell them the facts if they want to know. Even if they don't, they should be told and made to face up to it. If the 'tell nothing' school lacks sense and manifests stupidity, the 'tell all' lacks both sense and sensitivity.

There is bound to be a better way. It is when each person is dealt with individually, given time and space, taken at his own pace and allowed to assimilate the information, asking whatever questions he wishes, when he wishes. If it is countered that a consultant cannot afford the time to do this – although it is amazing how many can if it is being paid for privately – then let him delegate the responsibility to other members of his team. It is not good enough to leave the nurse on duty to cope with the patient's uncertainties or with the results of information given badly or uncaringly.

Comparing the difference in atmosphere between our large teaching hospitals and hospices, one is struck by the sense of frenetic activity in the one and quiet tranquillity in the other. There are obvious reasons for this – the hospital is geared to crisis intervention, the hospice is there for terminal care. Different situations require different skills. Yet when due allowance has been made for the factor, it still does not account for the different atmospheres. Could it be that part of the difference is explained by the fact that, along with the capacity for hard work, the humour which pervades and the humility practised – well, most of the time! – there is also an atmosphere of honesty?

Each one knows that whatever information asked for is given openly, his or her pace being the governing factor, and when a person needs space to take it in, he is not crowded out or left to face it alone. The attitude is: "Here we are, can we help you?" In the helping, the helper is also helped, the discoveries are made together, the difficulties jointly encountered and overcome. The ultimate in good patient care has happened – the patient too has been accepted as a member of the team, not just somebody to be 'done good to' but to be 'worked along with' as we journey towards the dawn.

Time

LOSS GIVES RISE to many paradoxes, one of which relates to time. The person who is dying is frequently conscious of the brevity of what is left of time. The person who has suffered loss is often only aware of how much of it lies ahead, with the unendurable emptiness associated with it. Those of us in a supportive role need to be aware of the significance of this.

Any healing process will take time. We must, however, be careful how we express that. Few things are more insensitive than to say: "Time will heal". It is insensitive in that each one knows this to be true – we either get better or worse, we are cured or we die, in which case time does not matter any more! What makes it so distressing is that, so often when it is said, the hearer has the feeling that in fact nothing will ever heal. It is that which makes it so terribly painful – the feeling of surrounding darkness and despair which does not go away, and the attendant anxiety that it never will. The well-intentioned friend who assures us that time will heal, only seems to rub salt into the wound. It certainly does not ease the pain there and then. Any loss takes time to be processed. Just as we can anticipate a delay of about nine to twelve months after surgery before we are fully 'at ourselves', so we must allow for a similar time span after a bereavement. For some it may not be as long, for others it can be a lot longer. What is being noted here is the fact, accompanied as it is by the bereaved person's vulnerability during the period. Because there are raw nerve ends and the person is emotionally fraught, we need to be on our guard against encouraging any action or reaction without allowing further time for reflection and response.

In dealing with ourselves we need to take time, and in dealing with others, to give it. Self-esteem takes a sharp knock when we encounter distress. We are diminished. When time is taken with a person, not only are they allowed to talk and express themselves, but they begin to feel they have some worth and dignity again. The quickest way to get rid of somebody is to look at one's watch – immediately there comes the response: "I'm sorry for using up so much of your time." To give time freely elicits the reaction: "She gave me the impression of having all the time in the world for me."

A widow who spoke in the highest terms of the professional care given by their general practitioner to her husband during his last illness told how she went to see him after her husband's death. He is a very good doctor who uses the appointments system. After her allotted seven minutes she was given a prescription for an increased number of anti-depressants. In reflecting on this she remarked that if only he had been prepared to give her five minutes more of a consultation he might have been able to reduce the medication. She would be the first to realise that this may be somewhat exaggerated, but in essence she was right. What she needed was time. She did not get it.

A minister who spends much of his day dealing with people in distress tells of a caller in obvious need who came to see him. For nearly three-quarters of an hour they sat together in total silence without saying a word. There were all the indications of strain. Finally the young man broke down and in a torrent of words the cause of the upset was spelled out. Some further time was spent in dealing with the problems before the caller left, relieved and composed.

Suppose the minister had grown weary after fifteen minutes and had said: "Come on, now, what's the bother?" he might well have got rid of his caller somewhat faster but he might also have sent somebody on his way more hurt, more wounded and more broken. There had to be the giving of time, the granting of space, the enabling silence – all of these were essential. All helped to create an atmosphere in which without haste or hassle the person in need was allowed to take his time to bring to the surface those things from deep within him which could not be summoned at a moment's call.

The chief complaint made about so many in the caring agencies is that "they are too busy, they do not have the time." It is a strange commentary on our society. Never was there a period when so many people were employed to look after other people, yet that same era had produced an organisation of unpaid volunteers like the

Samaritans, part of whose *raison d'être* is to be available to offer unhurried friendship to anybody who may need it at any time.

The playful cynic has suggested that in the story from which the organisation derives its name, the priest who passed by on the other side, and the Levite who came and looked on the man in distress, may both have been decent solid citizens, with good will and concern in their hearts, but they just did not have the time to do anything about the man in his need. They may even have been on their way to Jericho to set up a committee to do something about appointing a working party to look at safety measures for travellers on the Jerusalem to Jericho highway! With weighty matters like that on their minds it was no wonder they were unable to attend to the needs of an injured man. He could, after all, have been part of an elaborate ploy set up by people who weren't really worth bothering about in any case! Now if he had been one of their own kind, that would be another matter. It might have been a useful case study for the meeting. Think what that would have done for us all – given us a useful precedent on which to base subsequent practice! But we would have lost the priceless story of a certain Samaritan who made time to go where his neighbour was, and challenged us to do the same. He was not described as 'good' in the original story. Perhaps on this occasion the later gloss is justified.

Talk

ONE OF THE most frequent complaints which bereaved people make about how they are dealt with is the unwillingness of other people to allow them to talk about their loss, or to listen when they do so. Attempts are made to shut them up – "You'll only upset yourself by talking about it, dear" – which more accurately means: "You'll only upset me if you do!" Frantic efforts are made to avoid the topic of what has happened, even to the extent of avoiding people, crossing to the other side of the street, imagining it will not be noticed. It invariably is, adding even more hurt to the pain. The most significant event in a person's life is not talked about. Conversation about trivia is sustained lest the dreaded happening should be mentioned. Who really wants to talk about the weather or holidays when the heart is heavy with sadness and the tears cannot be stifled?

A widow spoke of her feelings after her husband died. Her family were supportive, but she got the impression after a number of months that they were getting fed up with her "going on about it". It did not help her to feel any better. One night it was so grim she phoned the Samaritans. The girl on the other end simply allowed her to talk, which she did for about two hours. The 'friendly stranger' listened. That was all she did, The caller was so relieved. At the end of the call she began to reflect on what had happened, how she had been helped by being allowed to talk to somebody who was willing to listen. She thought that if so much could be accomplished by something as simple as that, perhaps she might be able to do the same for others in the same or a similar plight. She offered her services as a volunteer in the local branch. She was accepted, and became an excellent worker as was evidenced by her presence at a conference on bereavement where she shared her story.

Bereaved people need the opportunity to talk. They are seldom given the chance to do so. The 'cop out' explanation given is that "we do not want them to be upset". The real reason, as I have already suggested, is that we are not sure how we could cope with their upsetting us. "Supposing I broke down and cried. I'd feel dreadful. I'm sure it would not help her in any way." But what right have we to say such things when we don't know? Is not the truth, rather that we back off because we are as much afraid of our own reactions as we are of the other person's?

A colleague whose husband committed suicide told how when it happened some of her friends could not say anything, so they didn't. Others said how shocked and upset they had been when they heard the news. They just could not take it in. They spoke at great length about their own feelings. Only one person actually asked her how she felt, and waited to hear a reply. She needed to talk. She wanted to do do. Only one was willing to listen.

Listening is the most neglected art of our age. Young people say of their parents, "They are good at giving me things, but not at giving me themselves when I need somebody to listen to me." In marital breakdowns much is made of the failure of communication. What seems to happen is not so much that partners have stopped talking to each other – they have stopped listening to each other.

A patient who had been in hospital for major surgery told how one day during his convalescence he met a friend when out walking. The friend asked him how he was. Before giving him an opportunity to reply, he mentioned that "he'd had a spot of bother himself". He had got a speck in his eye, it had been grim, he had had to have it seen to in hospital. He talked for half an hour about it before going on his way. He never heard how the surgery patient was, because he never waited to hear. That patient has since died of his terminal cancer. The man with the speck in his eye is still going strong.

People do not listen. They do not realise that one of the things which a person in distress needs most is the opportunity to spell out in detail what has happened, to talk it through. This is so often denied, with long-standing and damaging side-effects.

Encounters in hospital and pastoral practice have shown that people, given the opportunity and encouragement to talk, will tell of painful loss experiences in the past which happened years before which they have never been allowed to talk about. These experiences have been repressed, but recent events or pending surgery have activated them and brought them to the forefront of their thoughts. Given the opportunity to talk, given a ready, sympathetic listener, such people have found the comfort and release which they could not imagine would be possible just by talking. They have spoken of "a great burden being released", "a load off my mind", an easing of tension and a tranquillity and peace descending.

Listening like that requires concentration, the discipline of not interrupting, the avoidance of advice-giving with no preaching or pontification – all of which is a tall order for many professional carers and most clerics, who for all their skills as communicators are frequently very bad listeners! For those who are prepared to work at learning the art, the rewards are immense, not the least being not having to play at being God but just acting as an ordinary human being, like anybody else!

If people need to talk– as they so often have said they do – they may not be able to do so when the tragedy happens or the terrible event takes place. At the time they can feel so numbed that they are unable either to think clearly or talk coherently. It is often much later on that they need a listener. Then nobody is available.

She was a young married woman, in hospital for observation. When the chaplain came to see her he tried to make contact by finding out where she came from and some personal details. She told him she had a family. There were three children. There had been another daughter, but she was dead. The chaplain asked her about all the children including the one who had died. The mother talked freely and feelingly about them all, including Hilary, who had died six years before. He encouraged her to tell him about what had happened. This she did in great detail. She spoke of what she felt about the hospital where Hilary had died, how she had been dealt with, her disappointment, her anger with the doctors, with her family, her husband, herself and with God. It was a classic example of post-bereavement distress. When asked if she had ever talked about it before she said: "No. I would not talk about it at first, I was too shattered, but when I wanted to talk about it six months later, there was nobody to listen. Nobody wanted to know." If only somebody had picked up the longing for the listening ear, then there might not have been the hospitalisation six years later on – at least so the woman claimed. The chaplain who listened felt so, too.

A television documentary on the aftermath of the tragic events in Hungerford was both moving and reaffirming. Without prying, it allowed viewers to draw alongside the bereaved. It reaffirmed much that had been spelled out here and elsewhere about grief reactions. It showed again and again the need for people to listen to what the distressed were saying. It also indicated how much help was gained by those who are allowed to talk and encouraged to do so.

One interview with a married couple told of the effects of the tragedy on their lives. The wife had resented her husband talking to a counsellor about his feelings, and not to her. The help given by the counsellor was such that a bond developed between counsellor and counselled which nearly brought about a marriage breakdown. The couple had weathered the storm, but there was evident residual anger and misunderstanding. The wife was angry because her husband had not talked to her but to a stranger. The husband had misunderstood the personal dynamics between himself and his befriender. There had developed an emotional relationship which was a potential threat to the marriage. This couple were able to save the situation by working at it. But it does not always work out that way. Because of the risk factor, we do well to understand the dynamics a bit better.

Sometimes we find it easier to talk to an outsider rather than a close relative. This is not necessarily any reflection on relationships, but a recognition of a hidden anxiety. There is the fear that if the pain is spoken of to a wife or relative there might be misunderstanding, loss of face; we "mightn't be able to face him or her afterwards." Having uncovered the wound, one does not want it to be looked at again. The loved one, being distressed by it, might out of genuine concern keep asking about it, opening up the wound at an inappropriate moment. This sets up a vicious circle of: "Why did I tell her? Look how I've upset her. Maybe she'll not be able to accept me ever again as the person I was." So the distressed person, already in pain, afraid of the additional risk inherent in opening up to family, chooses to go to a stranger where there is not the same risk.

There are other risks not recognised when the process begins. To unburden one's soul to somebody who is caring enough to be available, willing enough to listen and who has no other expectations, is therapeutic. The sheer relief is such as to create a sense of gratitude to the listener, which unless carefully handled, can lead to complications as it clearly did in the example cited. To recognise what can happen and why is to be forewarned. It can be easier to speak to the friendly stranger who is seen only infrequently than to the family member who is encountered daily. Families need to understand that. It should not be resented or misunderstood. It is not necessarily any reflection on them or on their love. Equally, in availing oneself of such support there must be open acknowledgement of the dangers in the process. A skilled and sensitive monitoring of the situation can avoid pitfalls, leaving everyone enriched and no one impoverished – but it takes skill. The skills are taught to the trained counsellor, but not everybody remembers the techniques if emotions become involved at an unpredicted level.

Why is listening so important? There are many possible reasons, of which two are most frequently identified.

One is summed up in the words of a distressed person who told his befriender: "You are the first person who has actually listened to me. Everybody else has either lectured me or told me what to do. Nobody listened to what I wanted to say or wanted to hear how I felt. So many said 'If I were you', not realising that they weren't me. But you have listened to me and I am grateful." It may be that he overstated the position, but that was what he felt. The felt or perceived idea is frequently the dominant one. Nobody had ever listened to him. Nobody had taken him seriously.

The other stems from the fact that in listening to a person we are affirming his or her value or worth. We are by implication saying: "You really matter." In a world where many people feel they don't, that is very important. If you see yourself as only one very small cog in a huge industrial wheel, an insignificant unit in a multinational corporation, living with uncertainty about your future, threatened with the possibility of pay-off or redundancy if the outlet proves no longer to be viable, you have a sense of worthlessness. If you feel yourself to be just another patient described by a condition or known by your number, it undermines your sense of dignity and robs you of your identity. In these circumstances, to be listened to, to be given undivided attention, to hold centre stage, if only for a brief period, does something to counter all the other demeaning things which are happening. It helps to redress the balance which seems most of the time to be tipped on the side of the professionals, who talk about, but seldom to, the client. The talking is so often to elicit information, but not a consulting with the patient as a human being. When a person in need is listened to, he feels that some control of his destiny is still in his hands. That can be no bad thing for his morale and a positive aid to recovery.

Tears

" JESUS WEPT." The shortest verse in the Bible encapsulates the human response of a man of strength to a situation of distress. In an Eastern culture it would not have been thought inappropriate or strange. In Western cultures displays of feeling by men are generally considered to be taboo or out of place. For a woman to cry is permissible, but not for a man. It conflicts with the macho image expected of the male of the species. But why should this be?

There is a therapy in tears. A doctor writing of this drew attention to the statistical fact of female longevity. He speculated on the possibility of women's living longer being due to their greater willingness to cry than men. In the shedding of tears there is not only a release of tension but also of a toxic component. Instead of shoving the 'grief-poison' down into the system, it is being released. Men, with their inability to cry, damage their health. Women show greater wisdom, with attendant benefit to their physical well-being.

In rural Ireland to this day there is still a place for the 'wake'. It was and is the shared experience of bereavement. While doubtless there are excesses of behaviour which cause some church authorities to frown on the custom, there was great insight inherent in what was happening. There was the shared experience – social and religious barriers disappearing in the face of sorrow; the sharing of food and drink – for some having almost a sacramental dimension; the mixture of hilarity and sorrow, expressed in laughter and tears. All these elements have immense significance for those who "have eyes to see and ears to hear". The retaining of them is beneficial. The loss of them in the more clinical approach to death of modern urban society is detrimental.

The wake had a place for the 'keeners'. These were the people who orchestrated the weeping and wailing. Those who speak condescendingly of these things miss their profound meaning. The keeners who created an atmosphere in which tears could be shed, were performing a useful task and meeting a real need.

It would be a valuable exercise to look at the incidence of 'post-bereavement grief', as it is clinically described, in urban and rural settings. I have a feeling, albeit subjective at this stage, that grief would prove to be far less of a problem requiring medical attention and hospitalisation in a country community than a city setting. In the country, people are given the time and space to grieve. In the city, we are in such a rush that we have to get over it quickly and get on with living – but so often at what cost? The keeners are not figures of fun to be laughed at, but serious expressers of deep-felt pain which requires an outlet. Tears are a God-given medium. It is only male foolishness which fails to recognise this. Their avoidance can lead to a consequent delay in recovery, and bring about the necessity which some feel, that they have to apologise for them. (How odd to feel the necessity to apologise for our tears! We don't apologise for our laughter!)

Shared tears can have an even greater significance. They either bespeak, or create, a bond.

In the southern states of America during the days of slavery there were very close ties between some of the slaves and their masters and mistresses. That in no way justified a system which was an affront to human dignity, but factually reflected the situation as it was in some cases. In one such close relationship an onlooker remarked to a woman slave: "You and your mistress are great friends". To which she replied: "Oh, no, we ain't. We're not friends, we're only acquaintances. We ain't never cried together." Tears can create a bond. They are not, or need not be, a barrier.

Studies have been done which indicate clearly that the death of a child tends either to bond a marriage together or break it irreparably. Couples are either drawn closer or are pulled apart. When a break takes place it is often accompanied by an amalgam of pain, anger, guilt and blame. When it does not take place it is frequently because tears have been shed jointly. In the visibly shared sorrow has come an inwardly perceived reconciliation.

The book *Facing Life and Death*, edited by Harry Guntrip, tells the story of Leslie Tizard, a Congregational minister in Birmingham. At fifty-five years of age, without any prior indications, he was diagnosed as having cancer. He decided he would write about his response to his illness and his reactions to his gradually weakening condition. It is a most moving and illuminating account, written during the last four months of his life. In commenting upon the sheer strain and stress placed on Leslie and his wife, Harry Guntrip writes:

> There were things on the minds of each of them which they did not know whethcr to speak freely about, so that in a way they became afraid of each other. But with two people who were prepared fundamentally to be real with each other, this could not last and it did not. One day an incident occurred which enabled the ice to be broken. Leslie was speaking to his wife about his book on preaching which he had nearly completed. He began to express the wish that if he was unable to finish it, another minister should write a Foreword to it. At that point he suddenly broke down and wept, the tension disappeared and they could talk freely again. It was the shared tears which did it.

> There was another occasion, during his second stay in hospital, when he knew in himself he would not come out again. A TV set had been kindly installed in his room and while he and his wife were together a Christmas carol programme

began. It was too much for them and they wept together. Once again they realised that they had both been trying to 'be brave', and the over-control of emotions involved was beginning to isolate them from each other once again, The simple release of natural, if pent up, feeling brought them back in touch again. It was the shared tears which did it again. It cemented the relationship as so often it can do.

While this is all true, a note of caution needs to be sounded. We must avoid forced ritual tears. Some there are who cannot and do not weep easily or openly. They must not be made to feel odd because their response is not what is expected. Neither must it be assumed their non-display of emotions is an indicator of any lack of feeling. There are tears shed which are never seen, either because they are shed in private or because they are shed inwardly. To stereotype grief responses is insensitive to individuality and unfair to deeply felt feelings which are not necessarily expressed in ways interpreted as sorrow by others. Each person must be permitted to deal with his or her grief in the way which is appropriate to them. A forced conforming reaction is not genuine. The unreal response is no healthy way to come to terms with one of life's ultimate realities.

Trauma (Personal)

ALL LOSSES ARE uniquely personal because all persons are unique. No two are exactly the same, therefore the experiences we encounter are individual and personal albeit with domestic and social implications. We are individuals but we do not live in isolation. In that sense no two situations or events are comparable – although there may be common threads found in most of them and responses to them.

It is not to minimise the significance of any loss (it is after all "the bottom falling out of my world") to recognise the appropriateness of using the term 'traumatic' for some events. They are shattering. Those who work in the Samaritans know at first hand something of the traumatic impact of suicide on family and friends. No matter how well schooled one may be in the classic signals, when it happens there is shock. Knowing it is unpreventable if there is a total intent to terminate life, does not radically diminish the guilt feelings experienced by family, friends and other support persons. They still feel bad about it. They go over again and again the clues given and the cries for help expressed saying: "Why didn't I pick them up".

The things to look for are not always seen clearly although they are always obvious afterwards. They are worth identifying again. The Samaritan organisation lists thirteen danger signs of suicide risk –

- Caller withdrawn, cannot relate to you. Medical aid may be needed.
- Family history of suicide.
- Earlier attempts at suicide.
- Definite idea of how suicide would be committed. The tidying up of affairs indicates suicide is being planned.
- Anxious tone to depressive picture.
- Dependence on alcohol or drugs.
- Some painful physical illness and long sleep disturbance.
- Feeling of uselessness. In elderly, lack of acceptance of retirement.
- Isolation, loneliness and uprooting.
- The possibility of having to live with few human contacts.
- Lack of a philosophy of life such as a comforting type of religious faith.
- Financial worries.
- Within the period of the rise and fall in mood, the most dangerous time is often when the caller appears better. Now the caller has enough energy to kill himself or herself.

Sadly, despite all the efforts of the Samaritans and other agencies there has been an increase in the suicide and attempted suicide figures in this island. Young unemployed men between the ages of 15 and 35 are most at risk, just as more young women were liable to attempt suicide than men with a levelling out of these figures recently. Actual suicide or attempted suicide (sometimes spoken of as para-suicide) is rightly a cause for concern and there have been increasing indicators that the Government, medical and social services are becoming more actively involved in examining causes and attempting to be more pro-active to the situation to meet needs.

When the trauma actually happens there are for most people the usual reactions to loss. However, two frequently surface with even greater intensity – guilt and anger. The guilt is because of the missed clues and the missed opportunities. The pointers were either not observed or followed up. "I just didn't think he was serious." "He'd talked that way before." "She always was a bit dramatic." "Why didn't I pick up the signs and act upon them." "If I had he or she might have been alive today"! All the painful quotes are cries from the heart and expressions of a guilty conscience. Nothing can be done about it now save to aim to be more aware and alert when other not dissimilar situations occur.

The anger expressed (or sometimes repressed) is often with the person who kills himself. Not just: "Why did he do it", but "He's got off side and left me and others to cope with a right mess." "It's all very well for her but the family have to deal with getting on with life." "It was really very selfish of her – and I'm very angry not for myself but for others." It is important to let the bereaved express their anger without being judgmental about it. Apart from anything else none of us can be sure exactly how we would react personally if in a similar situation.

It is equally important to be there to help the person cope with the guilt feelings afterwards when he or she feels bad about the awful things said. "I didn't really mean them but I was so angry". To draw alongside and not to blame is to help the healing process on its way, although by the very nature of the event and the circumstances it may take longer and be a more difficult journey.

Trauma (Communal)

I F SUICIDE IS one of the traumas of which we have become more aware – with the attendant implications of that – the tragedies of the communal catastrophes created by the violence expressed in this island as a whole – for we do not forget the loss of life in Dublin and Monaghan – it is in Northern Ireland it has been most vividly witnessed in a collective sense. Remembering, because 'no man is an island', all loss will impinge on somebody's world. The carnage of The Abercorn, Bloody Friday, Bloody Sunday, Greysteel, Loughinisland, Enniskillen and Omagh were events which reverberated round the world not just as expressions of human bestiality but places where tragedy was writ large and has left scars which remain.

While wounds have for many healed for others they still remain and fester. Any community hurt, like Dunblane or the Hillsborough Football disaster or Stardust Ballroom disaster, opens up the wounds again, reactivating the feeling of hurt and brokenness.

New situations produce new skills or techniques – or possibly more correctly finer tuning of long-standing skills being reorganised and sometimes given new names! People used to be available to allow others to cry on their shoulders, having given a listening ear and a helping hand but now it is called 'counselling' for which courses are run and diplomas awarded. Indeed it is even being suggested by some that only those 'trained, qualified and recognised' should be permitted to be involved in any way in times of personal or national disaster. Whilst in no way depreciating the use of trained professionals, in that distressed people are especially vulnerable and potentially at risk, care needs to be taken not to imply that the 'milk of human kindness' can only be given from recognised dairies and that it must all be professionally pasteurised before it is safe for consumption.

"How did earlier generations manage?" – is sometimes asked. The professional would often imply that they didn't and that we are dealing with the casualties centuries later. Maybe so but we will not be round to see whether we have done better with our post-trauma teams and strategies descending on communities sometimes more confused by the profusion of attention and support available when it happens, but more confused and distressed when the teams have to move on to the next disaster to be available there. 'Leave it to the professionals' may be a popular adage. Incidentally who invented the phrase? Was it the professionals themselves? Many ordinary people have immense resources of courage and strength which emerge in crisis and many people show insight and compassion when just being good neighbours. (What training did the Samaritan have to prompt him to respond on the

Jerusalem to Jericho Road? It has been playfully suggested that Priest and Levite, later conscience-stricken about their non-involvement, got together to form a committee to look into the issue of Potential Casualties on that particularly dangerous stretch of the road. We still await their report! Meantime, the nameless Samaritan was getting on responding instinctively to the impulse to draw alongside people in need irrespective of class, colour or creed. Incidentally Jesus said "go and do likewise", not go and form a committee!).

This is not to denigrate the place and role of professional bodies but rather to underline the place of ordinary people being available to help ordinary people because that is what most of us are. To be treated with humanity and compassion and not as some statistic, or case study or thesis material is the simple plea of most of us. We want to feel that somebody cares personally about us – not because it is his or her job to do so but because we have significance and worth not just as a casualty but as a person.

One of the by-products of tragedies either personal or communal is media interest. The events and happenings of the global village are beamed into our sitting rooms via TV and screamed at us through newspaper headlines. What is happening in other parts of the world is on our own doorsteps within hours. It is not quite so pleasant when our doorstep becomes the showpiece of world news. People want to know – sometimes because they are interested, sometimes because they are inquisitive. Their interest span is not too long. People have a right to know because we are the inhabitants of one world and we belong to each other but the viewing can be voyeuristic and the information gathering intrusive. The offensive interview can have as long-lasting effects as a shrapnel wound. It is maybe for this reason we need to be protected, not so much from ourselves as from those who want us to emotionally undress ourselves in public. They may get a good interview – a good piece – but at what cost, as some of us know who have to deal afterwards with people angry with themselves for allowing themselves to be conned into "answering a few questions" which "will only take a few minutes" – but the effects can last a lifetime.

There are many journalists and media personnel who act responsibly. We pay tribute to them for their contribution. They have told our stories and we have been well served by many of them. Some who learned their trade here have gone on to gain international recognition. That is fair enough. What isn't fair is when there are invasions of privacy, with intrusive questions. People who have some experience of the media have knowledge of how to deal with them – although they too can become 'unstuck' – but the unprepared and uninitiated are not equipped to deal with journalists and interviewers.

We are all of us so vulnerable to flattery, being persuaded by well-known media channels that, instead of telling them to 'get lost', we invite them in and *we* get lost only realising it when they have gone and we see and hear what we said (or the edited bits) and are angry and embarrassed by it. On reflection we wish we'd never done it. When we are distressed we are very vulnerable, much at risk. When we have suffered loss we are in a state of shock and need to be careful of not only what we do but what we say. Once it has been said it cannot be unsaid. If we find it hard to protect ourselves and our privacy we need to be helped to do so, otherwise it may be gone forever.

A leading media personality said that some of the best interviews she had done she felt she couldn't use because she had asked herself would she have liked her own mother to be subjected to her set of questioning. If she was unhappy about it, she couldn't or wouldn't use it and didn't. She may have lost some wonderful interviews, but she maintained her compassion and integrity. In the long run those qualities are more important than any professional award or journalistic prestige which might have been obtained for a scoop which left behind a scar.

Touch

IF IN WESTERN culture we have hang-ups about tears we have even greater ones about touch. To reach out and touch somebody can be an act liable to misinterpretation, perhaps even leaving one open to a charge of sexual harassment. This possibility stems from our solitary associations of touch with sexual activity – the fondle, the caress, the kiss, being seen as the early overtures of love-making. As a consequence it can be hard to see it not as something sexual but potentially significant as a means of communication. Just as there is a therapy in tears, so there is a language of touch.

This is not to be confused with the 'groper' syndrome – the professional person who imagines he has some right to paw over people without recognising how offensive that can be; such behaviour is an invasion of privacy and rightly to be resisted. A person who believes in or practises that sort of 'grope therapy' needs to be dealt with firmly. However, such crude tactile displays and responses should not blind us to other gestures which can be an effective form of communication when there are no words to convey the deeply felt message from within.

It is interesting to note how often Jesus, the great Physician, touched people. His purpose was not only to bring healing but to identify with the sufferer. This was particularly appropriate when so many in his day would have interpreted sickness as being solely a result of sin. Touch was his way of breaking the sound barrier.

Our cultural inhibitions prevent us from reaching out to people, which is a pity – for their sakes as well as our own.

A young man severely wounded in a bomb explosion was taken to a hospital where he was treated with great care and skill. A minister who was a family friend visited him daily, sometimes praying with him and sometimes simply sitting quietly at his bedside. Often in the quietness, or when praying, he would reach out and hold the patient's hand. As the young man's medical condition improved, the screens were removed from around his bed. With the greater openness of the public ward, this touching and clasping of the patient's hand ceased, in part because the minister thought it might be a source of embarrassment to the patient, or an occasion of innuendo and snide comments from others. After some weeks the patient said one day: "When I was very ill you used to reach out and hold my hand. It meant a great deal to me. You have no idea what it did for me. It brought comfort, strength and reassurance. You have stopped doing it now and I'm sorry." His friend felt ashamed that the possibility of misunderstanding by nasty-minded people had broken a link which had been a source of such consolation.

An American friend spoke of the way people had expressed their sympathy when his adolescent daughter died. His Catholic friends said things like: "It's God's will. She'll be an angel now." His Protestant friends did not say anything.

They were stoically silent. But his Jewish friends took him firmly by the hands and then gave him a great big bear hug. He commented: "I knew that here were people who at the core of their being knew what suffering was all about". They were trying to show that, while they could not express their feelings as they wanted to, or say what they had wished, they were revealing through touch how much they cared and how they identified with his sorrow.

Visiting with Mother Teresa one of her homes for the dying in Bombay, we came to a patient who was near to death. She told us she did not know where he came from or what his religion was, but it was important to show him the love of Christ as his life came to a close. We spent some time with him in quietness. There were no words which we could exchange. He knew no English, we did not know his language or dialect. As we turned to go away, one of us went back, knelt down beside the patient and gently kissed him on the forehead. What was he doing? Simply trying, through the language of touch, to say to his unknown Indian brother: "You matter and we care." How else to bridge the cultural and language barriers but in a mode which over-leaps them all? That thoughtful gesture said more than any words could have done.

There is always the cowardice which causes us to be afraid that a gesture will be misunderstood. So we hold back. The heart says "reach out"; the head says "no." Obey the heart: take the risk. Life's chapter endings can be enriched by such expressions of humanity.

In the geriatric unit of one of our large hospitals the staff have taken to giving the patients teddy bears. It was noticed that some patients seemed to derive comfort from reminders of childhood. Those who had little dolls would cuddle them and talk to them. This prompted a regular visitor to suggest that an appeal be made to the public for old teddy bears so that they could be given to patients who had none. There was a warm response. Visitors now can see numerous patients happily fondling their teddies. Doubtless some cynical researchers will dismiss this as regression to childhood. May it not also be seen as a sad commentary on a society that often leaves its old to derive consolation from a soft cuddly toy; because that same society will provide material care but is often unwilling to show warmth expressed in a tactile response to isolation and loneliness?

A minister who used to conclude his visits to an elderly lady with a prayer and a kiss on the cheek tells how on one occasion, because of the pressure of time, he made a brief prayer and went quickly away. When he had gone the old lady turned to her companion and said: "He remembered the prayer but he didn't give me a kiss." She valued the former, but she needed the latter. When she had both she was content. Maybe she recalled her childhood picture of a Jesus who not only prayed with people but touched them too. The pious are frequently willing to display devotion but deny affection. Fully integrated caring makes room for both.

Thoughtfulness

ANY LOSS EXPERIENCE reveals both our vulnerability and our sensitivity. We discover that we are capable of being deeply hurt as well as greatly helped. What is true for us is also true for others. Perception is the watchword.

Many centuries before Jesus there lived a preacher called Ezekiel, who wanted to be effective in meeting the needs of others and understanding their problems. His means of achieving this is described in a pictorial phrase: "I sat where they sat" (Ezekiel 3:15). In identifying himself with them, he became one of them, and was then accepted by them. While it is not always possible physically to identify with others in an exact location, a creative imagination enables a drawing alongside which can provide the key to understanding and an insight into what is happening.

It was that sort of imagination which caused a lady doctor in a large teaching hospital to kneel beside the bed of an elderly partially-sighted patient, taking her hand in hers and talking to her, person to person, and not as physician to a patient. She did not have to do it that way. She was not taught to do it that way. It was not expected of her to do it that way. But she did. She not only put the patient at ease but engaged in a therapeutic relationship which was remembered long after the medicines and treatment were forgotten. It was an imaginative stroke of untaught caring.

In a society not totally uncaring we are at our worst in our treatment of the widowed. (How some hate the word 'widow', just as they are upset by the phrase which speaks of 'losing a husband', as though it was an act of gross carelessness.) They speak of the pain of being forgotten – "I'll be along to see you, dear," but nobody remembers to call. They speak of the hurt of isolation, of being left out of dinner parties and the social functions – "Do I pose such a threat, or do they not know what to do with me?" They speak of the sheer loneliness of having nobody to discuss things with, no arm around them in bed at night – not sexual deprivation, simply social isolation.

A widow told how when her husband, a well known public figure, died unexpectedly, everybody was very sorry. They expressed their sympathy profusely. But when Christmas came there was not one who thought of inviting her to the office party or, even more distressingly, wondered how she would manage with the children. Maybe they were all well-intentioned, or perhaps they simply did not think. No wonder another commented that while in the East widows were burned on their husband's funeral pyre, in the West they are forgotten. She felt that maybe the oriental custom, while apparently cruel and painful, was possibly more humane.

If this all sounds harsh, if it is pierced through with bitterness, it reflects the hurt feelings of those who have had the experience of loss thrust upon them by life. They did not ask for it to happen. They had no wish for it – but it happened. When it did they felt they stood alone. The loneliness nearly drove them to despair. After the pain had eased a bit, when healing had come to their wounded spirits, they might not have expressed their feelings with such viciousness and passion. When the wound was still open, the flesh raw, they lashed out in fury and anger. Who can blame them? Only those who have never felt their pain, or been where they were.

The other side of this which we need to see is the recognition of how much little gestures of thoughtfulness and good will can mean to people in distress. The post-funeral visits exemplified by the minister who used to visit every day for a week, every week for a month and every month for a year. If that sounds too mechanical, better that than total avoidance and business which does not make the time to call. The telephone call on the anniversary day; the invitation for a drink or a cup of coffee; the shared recollections of a happy event rather than avoiding talking of it because it might upset; all these can bring great comfort.

Expressions of kindness are not measured by their costliness but in terms of the thoughtfulness which stimulated them. In this respect, as in others, we must not "despise the day of small things". The little things are frequently remembered when the big expressions of socially expected displays of sympathy are forgotten.

How much can be accomplished by a little note or a letter of sympathy! Preaching away from home in another city, a minister told how at the end of the service a member of the congregation spoke to him warmly about his sermon. He then took out of his pocket a letter in a somewhat tattered envelope, and gave it to the preacher to read. The handwriting was familiar, the style recognisable. The man said: "That letter was written to me by your father when my father died." They had been business associates. He went on to say: "When I find the going tough and my heart is heavy with sadness, I take out the letter and read it again. It gives me courage and enables me to go on." The preacher, in reading the letter, realised that it had indeed been written by his father, who had himself died more than twenty-five years before. For over a quarter of a century, it had brought consolation and comfort. Yet it was "only a letter". Perhaps in these days of speedy communication and the spoken word we should make time again for the word which is written and can be retained. We cannot tell what cheer it may bring to somebody coping with a 'dark night of the soul'. We shall never know unless we are prepared to try. We shall never try unless we not only think about it – but do it.

Those of us who are in the caring professions

need to be always aware that our patients, our parishioners, our clients, have a right to expect from us standards of professional competency. We should feel guilty when we fail them. After all, are we not being financially rewarded for professional services rendered? We are but dutiful servants. When the extra mile is walked, the duty exceeded, the unexpected action done, then we shall know the joy experienced by all those who hear the words of Jesus: "Inasmuch as you do it to my brothers you do it to me." When the opportunity is missed, the chance to help avoided, no matter what explanations or excuses there are of not knowing, or not realising, or not thinking, then there are the strictures of condemnation which tell us that when we did not do it to his brothers, we did not do it to him.

"Forgive me, Lord, but I just didn't think . . ." He will forgive, if we really want his forgiveness. But it will show true penitence if we make amends and remember next time.

Theology

THEOLOGY MEANS 'A knowledge of God'. Though actual knowledge of him may for many be limited, the recognition of his being is for all of us a factor with which to reckon and to be included in our thinking.

School days are said to be the happiest in our lives. They can be. Much will depend on the pupil's ability and his relationship with the teacher. For those with limited ability the days are made tolerable by the extra-curricular activities and the prospect of long holidays!

Some students have an ability with things literary while having almost a blind spot about things numerate. For one such, algebra and its mysteries created panic. The usual schoolboy plots were of little avail. The problems remained unsolved. It was not so when the schoolmaster dealt with them. He would take the textbook, look at the problem, identify each factor by a symbol on the blackboard. Laying down the book he would then proceed to solve the problem. He always obtained the correct answer. He was never wrong. What was the secret of his success and the student's failure? The master was always right because he took account of every factor. None was left out. The student's error arose invariably from his leaving something out. No matter how he tried, he could not achieve success. He came to recognise that the cause of his failure was in the neglected factor. He may not have mastered the subject, but he gained an invaluable insight for living – neglect any factor in the problem and the answer cannot be worked out properly.

Personhood is made up of different elements. No longer is the three-fold division into watertight compartments of body, mind and spirit accepted as doing justice to the human personality. Faculty psychology is 'out'. Today we think in terms of the totality of being, various elements making up the whole, inter-relating, intermingling, impinging on each other. To do justice to ourselves and to others we have to take account of the whole. Specialists may deal in minute detail with parts, but the person who is concerned for wholeness has to be conscious of a person in his entirety. Medicine itself as a speciality is becoming more aware of this, hence the recognition of the psycho-somatic illnesses: psyche – the mind; soma – the body. The skilled doctor no longer thinks the answer lies entirely with him. He avails himself of and responds to the insights of other disciplines, making them available in the care of his patients. The equally skilled priest is sensitive to the entire needs of his flock. He or she does not try from his or her own resources to meet all the needs, but to be a facilitator. Recognising that the spiritual symptom may be hiding a psychiatric problem, he leads in that direction to obtain the best possible help for his parishioner/patient. He is exceedingly foolish if he tries to do it all on his own, unless along with his theological training he has also been trained in other disciplines. Amateur psychiatrists can be a dangerous menace – as can amateur theologians! These risks being recognised, all the factors must be allowed for before there can be a satisfactory resolution of any problem.

What bearing has this on the question of dealing with grief or loss? Clearly every factor must be taken into account. Too frequently we overlook or neglect one or more. The religious component cannot be left out. It will have greater significance for some than others, but it must not be overlooked altogether. If it is, we will come up with an incomplete and thus unsatisfactory solution.

There are carers who recognise this. They see the clergy as allies. Others (not without some justification) see them as a nuisance. Some want to call them in when nothing else can be done, to gather up the pieces. If carers are truly professional they will recognise the need for colleagueship in the interest of their patients and in the lessening of their own workload. If clergy are sensitive and wise they will avail themselves of the expertise and insights of others, not imagining that they know all the answers and that they alone have the solutions. We need deliverance both from the professional Jim-will-fix-it types and the religious with the Jehovah complex! Respect for each other, respect for the total personality – these are vital ingredients which, if overlooked, cause bother.

The spiritual dimension is an element in

personality to be recognised. It is not always of the same significance for everybody. Just as with all our appetites so with the religious one. Some people eat more food than others. They require to do so. Some have a greater intellectual hunger than their fellows. Music and art loom larger in some people's lives. Sexuality has a greater intensity for some human beings. So too with the religious appetite. There are people who require a great deal of spiritual nourishment. There are others who can do with very little. This is not stated as a judgment but as an observable fact of experience.

The sensitive carer recognises all this when dealing with others. Equally he is not 'puffed up' if his appetite appears to be insatiable, not does she feel guilty if she can manage on 'iron rations'. Each must work out what is appropriate for personal nourishment, and endeavour with delicacy to discover what is right for those in his care. The carer must never spiritually force-feed. Neither must there be neglect on the assumption that, because my needs may be minimal, those in my care should be denied what they need. I may not want what is, and should be, on offer. They have a right to a faith which is sufficient, appropriate and nourishing for them.

Soames Forsythe, the central character in the Galsworthy saga, remarked: "Life's emergencies reveal us". Loss is one of life's major emergencies. There is seen the real person, not the public image. The mask falls, albeit sometimes only momentarily for the skilled actor, but it does fall.

"The nakedness doth appear."

Jesus had another way of putting it. He talked about the person building his house on the rock rather than on the sand. When the storm comes the house on the sand has no firm foundation and so disintegrates. That built on rock has a foundation which withstands the crashing waves. It remains secure. It is not the building itself which is important so much as the foundation on which it is laid.

All this has implications not only for the sufferer but also for the carer. Perhaps the reason why some are afraid of death is because it can show whether the foundations of our lives are faulty or not. The reluctance of some clergy to be involved in the dying process may be due to a personal lack of 'a surge hope'. Lacking a living certitude, they are fearful of the searching question or the probing enquiry. Sooner than have to deal with it, they evade it altogether. This is not to suggest that we have to have the capacity to answer every question before being available – that would be an impossibility. What is required, is a framework of certitude big enough to contain the uncertainties; the maturity that can say, "I don't know, but the One I do know can sustain and see me through. He who is sufficient for me with all my frailties can be sufficient for you." We need the bigness of faith that can acknowledge, "It is a terrible storm about which I am apprehensive. I don't know when it will blow over, or what the outcome will be, but the rock remains firm and secure." When such is the carer's faith he or she can be supportive without being intrusive, caring without being claustrophobic, and a source of strength to those who, fearing the storm, are reaching for an anchor firm and sure.

Pope John XXIII was visited once by a journalist who in the course of the interview, because of the pontiff's age, asked him how he felt about dying. The Pope, with a twinkle in his eye said: "My bags are packed and I'm ready to go." Happy it is for those for whom that is a personal reality. The role of the carer then is simply to wish the traveller *bon voyage*. The task is a lot harder when dealing with those whose packing is incomplete, who may not wish to go or who have decided to go early.

What matters is to be available in the way that is appropriate and helpful to the traveller, knowing that journey's end is ultimately in the hands of God and we are not held responsible for that. We are, however, accountable for the quality of care along the way.

Epilogue

I T WAS AT yet another conference. A young doctor came up to me and told me that his wife had been at a refresher course at which two sessions had been on the theme of this book. She had made some kindly comments about the content, having actually remembered some of it in quoting it to him. He noted the recurring 'T's.

He suggested another possibility: "How about tea? Don't overlook its usefulness. It can be a great help for distressed people." He was being serious. He was not being flippant. Come to think of it – there's something in it. Perhaps that is why, although some may scathingly dismiss all that I have written as "offering T and sympathy", to those who are prepared to take it all seriously it can make a highway of happiness through many dark valleys. To have done that, even for some, will have made the effort worthwhile.

Useful Numbers

Sources of support can be found in Churches, Social Services and Welfare Services in hospitals and local communities. There are bereavement counselling services in the following places:

Northern Ireland
Cruse Bereavement Care:

Armagh & Dungannon	(028) 8778 4004
Banside	(028) 2563 0900
Belfast	(028) 9043 4600
Causeway	(028) 2766 6686
Foyle	(028) 7126 2941
Newry and Mourne	(028) 3025 2322
North Down and Ards	(028) 9127 2444
Omagh & Fermanagh	(028) 8224 4414

Remember our Child:
Support for those who have lost a child (028) 9079 7975

Samaritans NI:

Ballymena	(028) 2565 0000
Bangor and North Down	(028) 9146 4646
Belfast	(028) 9066 4422
Coleraine	(028) 7032 0000
Craigavon & Portadown	(028) 3833 3555
Londonderry	(028) 7126 5511
Newry	(028) 3026 6366
Omagh	(028) 8224 4944

Bereavement Counselling Service for children:
Barnardo's	(028) 9040 3000

WAVE Trauma Centre:
Support for those bereaved or traumatised through the 'Troubles' in Northern Ireland

Belfast	(028) 9077 9922
Armagh	(028) 3751 1599
Londonderry	(028) 7126 6655
Omagh	(028) 8225 2522
Ballymoney	(028) 2766 9900

Republic of Ireland

Bereavement counselling
Good Shephard's Pastorial Centre   (01) 8391766

Bereavement counselling for children and young people
Barnardo's, Cork   (021) 4 552100
Barnardo's, Dublin   (01) 4732110

Bereavement by suicide
Irish Friends of the Suicide Bereaved, Cork
                                    (021) 4 316722
Northside Counselling, Dublin   (01) 8484789

Bereaved parents
Parents Alone Resource Centre, Dublin
                                    (01) 8481872
Irish Widower and Deserted Husbands, Dublin
                                    (01) 8552334
National Association of Widows in Ireland, Dublin
                                    (01) 6770977

Sudden infant deaths, stillbirths and abortion
Irish Sudden Infant Death Association
                                    (01) 8726056

Samaritans
Athlone   (092) 73133
Cork   (021) 4 271323
Drogheda   (041) 9 843888
Dublin   (01) 8727700
Ennis &Clare   (065) 6829777
Galway   (091) 561222
Kilkenny & Carlow   (056) 65554
Limerick & Tipperary   (061) 412111
Newbridge & Kildare   (045) 435299
Sligo   (071) 42012
Kerry   (066) 7122566
Waterford and the South-East   (051) 872114